Book of

Angels

The
Book of
Angels

Turn to your angels for guidance,
comfort and inspiration

Francis Melville

FAIR WINDS

PRESS

BRIGHTON, SUSSEX

A QUARTO BOOK

QUAR: TBA

Conceived, designed and produced by
Quarto Publishing plc
The Old Brewery
6 Blundell Street
London N7 9BH

10 9 8 7 6 5 4 3 2 1

ISBN 1-931412-83-9

Editor: Nadia Naqib
Senior art editor: Sally Bond
Designer: Trevor Newman
Text editors: Andrew Armitage,
Marie-Claire Muir
Assistant art director: Penny Cobb
Picture Research: Image Select International
Photographer: Michael Wicks
Illustrator: Sally Cutler
Indexer: Dorothy Frame
Art Director: Moira Clinch
Publisher: Piers Spence

Fair Winds Press
33 Commerical Street
Gloucester, MA 01930
USA

Sheridan House
112–116A Western Road
Hove, East Sussex
BN3 1DD
ENGLAND

The Book of Angels

Manufactured by
Regent Publishing Services Ltd, Hong Kong
Printed by Midas Printing Ltd, China

Copyright © 2001 Quarto Publishing plc

Contents

Right: *Angel Standing in Storm* by Joseph Turner.

Introduction

The idea of spirits mediating between gods and mortals is a part of almost every traditional belief system that we know of. It is as old as the gods themselves. Nearly all the great religions have preserved this tradition in their teachings.

Angels in Tradition

h induism has its *devas,* semidivine spirits serving the supreme beings, while Buddhism has *bodhisattvas,* not spirits as such, but perfected people who delay entering nirvana to help others from beyond the material plane. The deities of pagan pantheons are comparable in their roles to the general concept of angels. The idea of guardian angels—spirits that are with individuals throughout their lives—may be the oldest angelic concept of all and exists in all traditional cultures. This book is mainly concerned with the angel traditions, esoteric and orthodox, of the great Semitic religions—Judaism, Christianity, and Islam— which share ancient roots, being drawn from the older traditions of the Babylonians, Zoroastrians, Assyrians, and Chaldeans. They conceive of angels as winged spirits mediating between Heaven and Earth. The recent upsurge of interest in angels has mingled tradition with New Age concepts, creating a new outlook, which regards angels as purely spiritual beings, who can manifest in any form. They were created by the Divine Source to sustain the light of Creation, and may be asked to assist us in all areas of our lives and to intercede with the Creator on our behalf.

The Study of Angels

From a scholarly perspective, angelology (the study of angels) is a highly complex field. While it is remarkable just how many similarities there are to be found, there are nevertheless many contradictory systems devised by mystics and theologians over the centuries. You can find scholarly works that explore some of these in exhaustive detail, but in order to establish your own connection with the angelic realm it is necessary only to understand the essential principles regarding the angelic hierarchies, their functions, and the leading angelic personalities.

Left: *The Angel of the North,* steel sculpture with the wingspan of a jumbo jet that stands on a small hill in Gateshead, England.

Angelic Existence

This endlessly mysterious life we find ourselves with is a long and often hard road. But if we sustain the idea that the universe is benign and the experience of life ultimately positive, then we can't go far wrong. The angels are here to help. All we have to do is ask. This, of course, requires faith. You have to accept the reality of angels in order to connect with them. If you have difficulty accepting that God created the angels to sustain the Universe and help humanity, which is the traditional view, then you may wish to explore other explanations.

Above: An illustration from an Arab manuscript showing an angel weighing souls.

Perspectives

The eighteenth-century visionary Emmanuel Swedenborg believed that the angels were perfected men and women (like the Buddhist *bodhisattvas*): "There is not a single angel ... who was originally created as such, nor any devil in hell who was created an angel of light and afterwards cast down thither, but all, both in heaven and hell, are from the human race." A Jungian perspective might be that angels are powerful psychological archetypes that have been given form by being believed in for thousands of years. In the end it is the individual heart, not the rational mind, that establishes a relationship with angels. A question often asked is, "If the angels are here to help us, why do they have to be asked?" The idea is that angels cannot interfere with our free will.

Above: We can call upon angels to watch over and help us, but they cannot interfere with our free will.

If we do not choose to engage with them they remain an abstract idea. However you choose to look at it, the pages that follow outline one of the greatest stories ever told. We will meet some of the best-known angels and establish simple rituals, including prayers, to invite them into our lives.

The ANGELS
—
ORIGINS & hIERARChY

‏❧

Tradition tells us that God created the angels on the second day of Creation. They were given the purpose of ministering to all the manifest phenomena in the Universe. But they did not come into existence to perform exactly the same functions. In the following pages you will find out about the angelic hierarchies and all the best-loved and most important characters in the angelic realm.

The **Nature** of **Angels**

❦

Before we explore the traditional origins of the angels, perhaps we should attempt to answer a key question: What is an angel? There are, of course, many definitions, but the general consensus is that an angel is an intelligence without a physical form, a purely spiritual being.

Angelic Governance

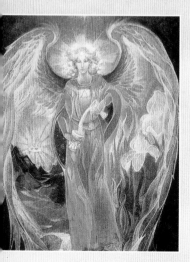

Left: Archangel Uriel, Angel of the Presence, pouring divine grace from the heavenly cup.

Unlike humans and all the species of animals on Earth, angels are not an evolutionary race. They were born perfect, fully capable of carrying out their functions. The only development they are traditionally accorded is the ability to learn from the experience of observing the Universe unfold. Angels govern everything. Their object is to sustain the whole of Creation. Every type and species of animal, plant, and mineral has an angelic intelligence behind it, as do planets, stars, and winds. Free from the restrictions of time and space, angels can move faster than the speed of light—they can be anywhere the moment they want to be—and they can assume any form they wish. Although neither male nor female in a reproductive sense, many tend, energetically, to one polarity or another.

The angels were given free will at the moment of their creation, but the majority voluntarily returned this gift in adoration of their Creator. Who needs free will when you can align yourself with the all-loving, all-knowing Almighty?

Above: In order not to confuse us, angels often manifest in the familiar form of beautiful floating beings with wings.

Light and Darkness

Hildegard of Bingen, a Bendectine abbess in the Rhineland area of Germany, and one of the greatest geniuses of the twelfth century, says that the angels are happy to serve and protect mankind because they are amazed by us:

> "All the angels are amazed at humans, who through their holy works appear clothed with an incredibly beautiful garment. For the angel without the work of the flesh is simply praise; but the humans with their corporeal works are a glorification: therefore the angels praise human work."

Angels can do nothing other than serve and praise God. The protection they gladly give us is against the machinations of the fallen angels. These are the angels who retained their free will. They wanted all the power and glory to themselves—not to serve but to be served. Their arrogance and envy undid them: they became devils, demons, fiends. As they hide in the darkness, their sole motivation is to undermine the harmony of the Universe. Thus all of humanity is engaged in the great battle between light and darkness, love and hate. So how did this whole story begin?

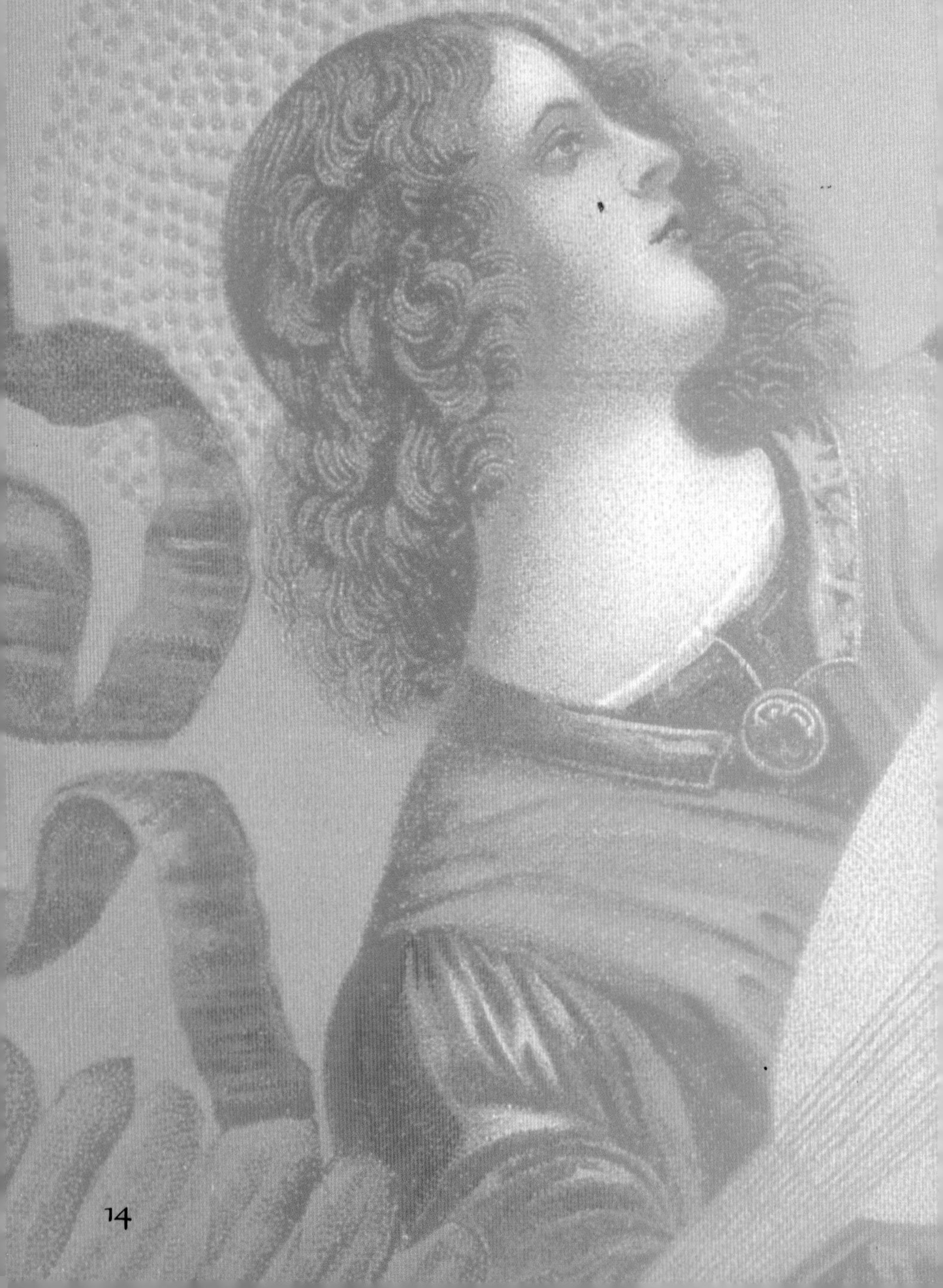

Creation

Most great spiritual traditions tell a story of Creation in which an eruption of creative power from another realm gives rise to the Universe as we know it. In the *Kabbalah*, the main strand of the Jewish mystical tradition, and one of the richest sources of angel lore, there is a beautiful and compelling version of the Creation story. This expands upon the version given in *Genesis* and has uncanny parallels with modern scientific theory. God is described as the Divine Presence, an omnipotent, indefinable, formless being in the midst of nothingness. When the One decided to manifest itself in form, the very idea created light. Then God "separated the light from the darkness," creating the first polarity. The material universe is defined by polarity—light and dark, male and female. Through this separation, the One became Two.

Then God, the Two in One, condensed his masculine aspect into a single tiny point of light. This is the "Word," the "Logos," the inseminating principle, which is then received by the "waters of the deep"—the darkness, the womb, the feminine aspect of God, which conceives and gives birth to the manifest universe.

Astrophysicists generally concur that the Big Bang occurred when a single point of incredibly condensed matter exploded to form the Universe as we know it.

Above: healing angels attend the efforts of a doctor to cure a sick patient.

The Shekinah

This feminine aspect of God, the Mother of the Universe, is known in Jewish tradition as the Shekinah. According to this tradition, she is God the Mother, the consort of God the Father. She is the divine radiance, the Great Mother who gives birth to the Universe. All feminine deities are aspects of her, as is the Virgin Mary. She is also described in the *Kabbalah* as the "liberating angel" and what Jacob in *Genesis 48:16* refers to as "the Angel which redeemed me from all evil." She is also the guardian of the Tree of Life in the Garden of Eden. Gershom Scholem, a great scholar of Jewish mysticism, tells us that the Shekinah was separated from her lover, God the Father, following the fall of Adam and Eve. Only on Friday nights, the Holy Night before the Sabbath, are they reunited before being forced to part again. Not until all the original light of Creation has returned to its divine source will the Cosmic Lovers be permanently reunited. Scholem writes: "to lead the Shekinah back to God and to unite her with Him is the true purpose of the *Torah*."

To the mystics of the *Kabbalah*, we are all involved in this process. Every act of love and compassion brings the heavenly couple closer together. In this sense life is a love story. In essence we are all lonely lovers separated from our love, which can be found only in our own hearts. The Shekinah is the Angel of Love, blessing and delighting in the union of lovers, which brings her closer to her own true love.

Above: The Tree of Life of the
Kabbalah. Right: Like the
Blessed Virgin Mary, the
Shekinah prays incessantly
on behalf of humankind.

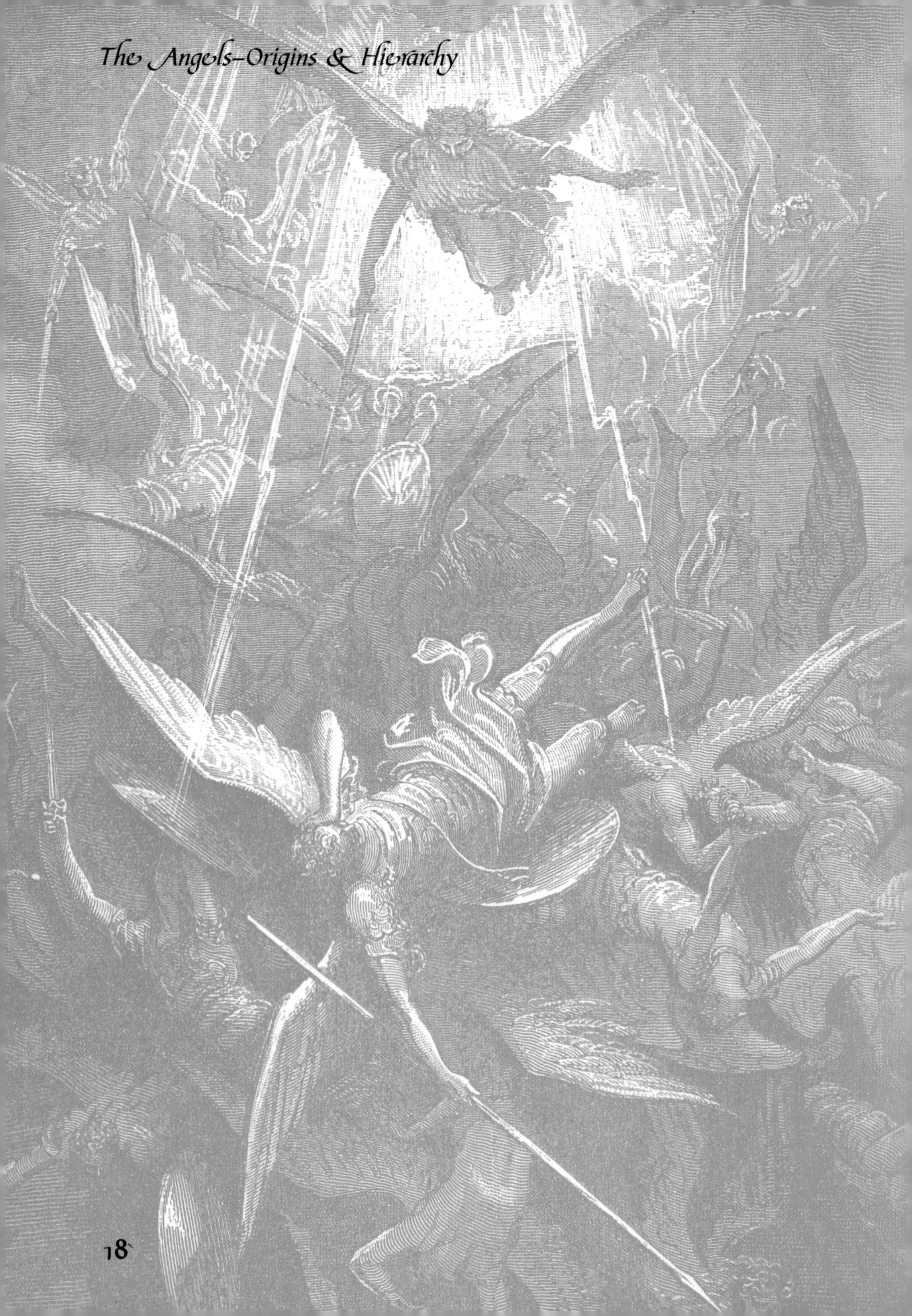

The Birth of the Angels

❧

The birth of the angels and mankind is recorded in more or less fragmentary form in various ancient texts. Most of these are Judaic and include the biblical book of *Genesis* and other writings, such as the *Apocrypha* and the *Pseudepigrapha,* which include much information on angels. Most of the Apocryphal texts are included in the Catholic version of the Bible. Later Judaic and Christian texts further fleshed out the story. From all these different sources can be woven the story of Creation, the War in heaven, and the Fall of Man.

According to ancient Jewish tradition the angels were the first intelligent beings created by God, and it is usually believed that they were all created in the same moment on the second day of Creation. God granted the angels free will, immortality, and divine intelligence.

The task they were offered was to sustain the Universe and reflect the glory of God. Most of the angels aligned themselves with the Divine Will and, to show their adoration, surrendered their free will to God. Those angels who did not, eventually succumbed to pride and came into conflict with God.

The War in Heaven

Thus began the War in Heaven, the story of which was greatly embellished by Jewish and Christian theologians in the early centuries after Christ. Satan, the

Devil, was conceived as having originally been a great angel in Heaven. He was given the pre-Fall name of Archangel Lucifer, based on a misinterpretation of a passage in *Isaiah*. One version of Lucifer's story tells that he was God's favorite angel, the most radiant in heaven (Lucifer means "lightbearer"), who refused God's command to bow down and honor Adam, the first man, as the image of God. Another version says that Lucifer was so proud that he seized an opportunity to sit upon God's throne. The incorruptible Archangel Michael took up

Left: The Archangel Michael vanquishes Satan and the rebel angels with the Sword of Truth and the Scales of Justice.

arms against him at once, whereupon he withdrew and gathered the support of a third of the angels of Heaven.

The titanic battle that followed led to the rebellious angels being thrown into the abyss as devils and demons.

The Fall of Man

Above: Adam and Eve are expelled from the Garden of Eden by the Angel of the Lord.

Mankind, then represented by Adam and Eve in the Garden of Eden, presented Satan with the best opportunity for revenge. According to one account, Satan disguised himself as a cherub and tricked the Archangel Uriel into telling him the way to Eden. In the form of a snake he slipped past the angels guarding the gates and found Eve on her own. He persuaded her to eat the fruit of the tree of knowledge of good and evil, which had been forbidden them by God. Thus deceived, Eve did eat, and gave Adam the fruit and he ate it, too. Their "eyes ... were opened, and they knew that they were naked." For the first time they knew shame and guilt and were fearful of God. This was the original sin, whence all man's troubles began. Expelled from the Garden of Eden, we have been trying to work our way back to Paradise ever since.

Thus we can see that the fall of mankind mirrors the fall of Satan and the rebel angels. Satan's sin is pride, whereas mankind's is shame. It was the shame—the sense of guilt and fear—that separated us from God. Adam knew he had done wrong because he felt embarrassed. He had developed a conscience and it is through conscience that we define our personal morality, our own knowledge of good and evil.

Choirs of Angels

The concept of an ascending hierarchy of different orders (or choirs) of angels is common to all traditions of angelology. There is a variety of versions regarding the names and the number of choirs. The best-known Christian version was devised in the sixth century by Dionsyius the Pseudo-Areopagite, a Syrian monk, who elaborated this system in his work, *The Celestial hierarchies*. This became established in mainstream Western culture as the classic work on the subject, and was adopted in the epic angel sagas of Dante and Milton. This system consists of nine choirs grouped in three triads.

Left: Choirs of angels eternally sing the praises of the Lord.

The First Triad

Seraphim

The highest-ranking choir of angels is the Seraphim, the "Burning Ones," whose light is so intensely bright that it would instantly incinerate mortals. These Angels of Love, Light, and Fire fly around the throne of God singing the Trisagion, a hymn of praise meaning "Holy, Holy, Holy." They absorb and reflect the divine light of God onto the next choir. Their regent princes include Seraphiel and Metatron.

Cherubim

The chubby baby cherubs we are familiar with from Renaissance art are a far cry from the mighty Cherubim, who rank as the second choir of angels. They are second in awesome radiance only to the Seraphim and reflect the knowledge and wisdom of God. In the Old Testament they guard the gates of Eden following the Fall. There were two carved Cherubim on the Ark of the Covenant, the fearsome secret weapon of the Israelites. Their chiefs include Kerubiel and Ophaniel.

Thrones

The Thrones are the "many-eyed wheels of fire" of the Merkabah, the Holy Chariot, circling the throne of God in unison with the Cherubim. They reflect faith in the power and glory of God and are said to reside in the Fourth Heaven. Their ruling princes include Tzaphkiel and Oriphiel.

Below: The prophet Elijah ascends to heaven in a chariot of fire, witnessed by his son Elisha.

The Second Triad

Dominions

Also known as Dominations, Lords, or, in Hebrew lore, the Hashmallim, the angels of this choir are said to aspire to greater grace and reflect the desire to transcend earthly values. They inhabit the level where the spiritual and physical planes begin to merge and are said to regulate the duties of the angelic choirs below them. Their ruling chiefs include Zadkiel, Zachariel, and Terathel.

Virtues

The Choir of Virtues is responsible for the motions and cycles of all the stars and planets in the Universe. They govern all natural laws and are therefore responsible for all miracles that break these laws. Known in the *Kabbalah* as the Malachim or Tarshishim, they reflect the ideals of virtue, inspiring valor in heroes and grace in saints. Their regents include Barbiel, Sabrael, and Hamaliel.

Below: Angels of the Choir of Powers guide a lost soul to heaven.

Powers

The angels of this choir are responsible for guarding the pathways leading to Heaven and for guiding lost souls onto these paths. They keep the world in balance and constantly defend against demons. They are granted authority to both punish and forgive and it may be they who deliver the "wake-up calls" we sometimes need to change our ways. They reflect the desire to resist evil and do good. Camael and Verchiel are among the chiefs of the Powers.

The Third Triad

Principalities

The angels of the seventh choir guide earthly rulers, leaders, nations, and all communities. They work with the guardian angels to inspire responsibility in individuals and can intercede in the affairs of humanity in ways that are not usually noticed. They are also said to be responsible for guiding religions in the way of truth. Cerviel is one of the ruling princes of this choir.

Archangels

The Archangels are the herald angels of God, appearing to people with messages and decrees from on high, as Gabriel did to the Virgin Mary, and to Mohammed to dictate the *Koran*. These are the angels most often seen by people, the guardian angels generally remaining invisible. They also intercede on our behalf, seeking forgiveness for our sins. Typical in this respect is the Virgin Mary, who became an archangel following the Assumption. The best known princes of this choir are Michael, Raphael, Gabriel, and Uriel.

Above: The Archangel Gabriel announces to Mary the Lord's will that she bear the holy Child. The white dove represents the holy Spirit.

Angels

The lowest order of angels is the one most involved with humanity, guiding and protecting us. These are the angels that keep cars on the road and generally prevent accidents and disasters as far as possible. They cannot interfere with our destinies, but, the more we ask for their help, the happier our destinies are likely to be. This choir includes the guardian angels and is ruled by Adnachiel.

The Seven heavens

Above: The Garden of Eden is said to lie in the southern half of the Third heaven.

The idea that there are seven heavens, not one, is an integral part of Jewish, Christian, and Islamic tradition. We still use the expression "to be in seventh heaven," to mean "as happy as can be," which makes sense because the Seventh heaven is the realm of highest perfection, the place where God resides. The tradition is very ancient, going back some 7,000 years to the Sumerian civilization of Mesopotamia, which spawned the Babylonian and Chaldean cultures, which were in turn hugely influential in the development of Near Eastern angelology. We can imagine the Seven heavens as a series of seven concentric rings with the Earth at their center.

First Heaven

Known as Shamayim or Wilon in Hebrew, its ruling angel is Sidriel. The First
Heaven contains everything in the three-dimensional Universe, the physical plane
of being. All the angels that rule the stars, planets, and natural phenomena such as
weather inhabit this realm, including the four Great Archangels—Michael, Gabriel,
Raphael, and Uriel—in their roles as planetary rulers.

Second Heaven

The Second Heaven is called Raquia and is ruled by the Angel Barakiel. This realm
is considered a holding ground for sinners awaiting Judgment Day. Some of the
fallen angels are imprisoned here, including those said to have had illicit relations
with the women of Earth. Islamic tradition holds that Jesus Christ and John the
Baptist reside here. Zachariel is one of its ruling princes.

Third Heaven

The regent Prince of the Third Heaven, known as Shehaqim, is Baradiel. In the
southern half of this realm lies the Garden of Eden and the Tree of Life, guarded
here by three hundred angels of light. It is here that manna, the heavenly nectar that
sustained the Israelites on their wanderings in the desert, is produced
by celestial bees. In the northern regions of Shehaqim lies
Hell and all its horrors, which may seem strange, but is
in keeping with the ancient notion that Heaven and
Hell lie side by side.

Fourth Heaven

The Fourth Heaven, called Machonon, is ruled
by Zahaqiel. It is home to "the heavenly
Jerusalem," the holy Temple and the Altar of God.

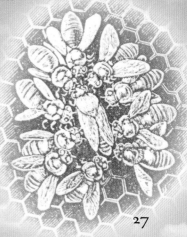

Left: The Archangel Michael
is the ruler of Araboth, the
Seventh heaven.

Fifth Heaven

Chief of the Fifth Heaven, Maon or Mathey, is Zadkiel, or, by some accounts, Sandalphon. As in the Second and Third Heavens, some of the fallen angels, notably the Grigori, or "Watchers," formerly the Guardians of the Towers of the four directions, are held. According to a vision of the prophet Zephaniah, a group of angels called the Lords, members of the Choir of Dominions, also reside here.

Sixth Heaven

Archangel Gabriel is usually recognized as Regent of Zebul, the Sixth Heaven. It is here that records are kept of all the happenings on Earth, natural events, and the deeds of individuals. These are studied by angels along with many other subjects, including astrology and ecology. Seven phoenixes and seven cherubim are said to dwell here.

Below: The Seventh heaven is the highest of all the heavens and the abode of God the Father.

Seventh Heaven

The highest of the heavens is called Araboth, ruled by the Archangel Michael, or, possibly, Cassiel. This is the abode of God and the highest orders of angels, the Seraphim, Cherubim, and Thrones. It is said that the spirits of human beings not yet born dwell in this realm. The Prince of the Divine Law, Zagzaguel, also resides here.

29

The Archangels

The Great Archangels include the best-loved
personalities in the angelic realms, but there is some
confusion in angelology as to who they really are and
what their roles are. This problem stems from the
very term *archangel,* which can refer to any angel
above the lowest-ranking choir. Thus, in a sense,
the mighty Cherubim and Seraphim are archangels,
but the Choir of Archangels
in Dionysius's hierarchy is the
second-lowest ranking of the nine.

Further, how can Archangel
Michael be a member of the
Choir of Archangels and also
a prince of the Seraphim, as some
authorities state? This apparent
inconsistency may stem from the
possibility that the archangels are the
most radiant beings that appear to
humanity. An angel of any greater
light than, say, Michael would be too
bright for mortals to behold without
being blinded. When the angelic
hierarchies were formulated by
Christian mystics like Dionysius,
therefore, it was assumed that
Michael must belong to one of the
highest choirs, because he appeared
to receive his orders direct from

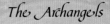

Left: The Great Archangels are among the best-loved of the heavenly hosts.

God. Also, as the vanquisher of Satan, Michael must surely be the most powerful angel of light in Heaven, given that Satan was supposed to have been a serious rival of the Most High. As for how many archangels there are, the consensus is seven, although the Christian churches recognize just two. Occult angelology elevates four archangels above the rest as the Angels of the Four Winds and the Four Elements. This forms the basis for the angelic equivalent of a "Wheel of Power," or Native American Medicine Wheel, probably the most fundamental ritual known to man, and integral to traditions the world over. A further three archangels make up the "Planetary Angels." There are many different lists of the seven archangels, but they all include Michael and Gabriel, the majority include Raphael, and the next most popular choice is Uriel. These are termed here as the Four Great Archangels.

The *Archangel Michael*

Fiery Prince of Light and Champion of humanity

Michael is probably the best known of all the angels, mentioned by name in the Old and New Testaments and the *Koran* as an archangel. His name means "Who is as God," a perfect reflection of divine light. He is the Prince of Light, leading the forces of good against the powers of darkness. Conqueror of Satan in the War in Heaven, he will lead the heavenly hosts in the final conflict. It was Michael who rescued Daniel from the lions' den and, according to Christian tradition, he antagonizes Satan by visiting each soul at the moment of death and offering the opportunity of redemption. Muslim lore descibes him as having wings covered with saffron-colored hairs, each of which has a million faces with a million mouths, all imploring God to have mercy on humanity.

32

Michael is the Dragonslayer, the heavenly counterpart of St. George. This is often thought to represent the triumph of Christianity over paganism, but in fact is rather the triumph of divine order over the chaotic powers of darkness. The most warlike of the archangels, he has appeared during battles, most memorably at Mons during World War I, when an overwhelmingly superior German army was inexplicably put to flight. German prisoners from the battle described a phantom army over the Allied lines, led by a resplendent figure on a white horse.

Associations and Symbolism

I n alchemical terms Michael represents the golden lion, the transmuted and perfected energy of the base primordial dragon. He is the patron of high places, and many hilltop churches in Europe are dedicated to him, usually as Saint Michael. The term *saint* reflects the ambivalence towards angels in Christian tradition.

Michael is guardian angel of both the Roman Catholic Church and the state of Israel. In art he is most often depicted wearing red and green, white, or shining armor. As Dragonslayer he wields sword or lance with his foot on the dragon's neck, and as angel of death and divine justice he holds a pair of scales. As Archangel of the South he represents the element of fire and the season of summer. He is best visualized in the fiery colors of red.

Left: In this woodcut for Durer's *Apocalypse*, Michael leads the warrior angels in the war against Satan and the forces of evil.

33

The Archangel Gabriel

Angel of Annunciation, Resurrection, Mercy, and Death

The great messenger angel, Gabriel is one of only two angels mentioned by name in the New Testament, the other being the Archangel Michael. The name Gabriel is derived from *gibor* and *el*, meaning "power of God." Gabriel is the Angel of Annunciation, who announced to the Virgin Mary that she would bear the Son of God, and to Zechariah that his wife Elisabeth would give birth to John the Baptist. Thus Gabriel is the Angel of Childbirth and of Hope, traditionally petitioned by women hoping to conceive, and has special duties regarding childbirth, guiding unborn souls throughout the nine months of gestation. The cleft between nose and upper lip is said to be the mark of Gabriel, where he touches the baby to admonish it to silence on the Sacred Laws. Following the darkness of death, Gabriel is again on hand to assist the soul to its rightful destination. He is often depicted blowing a trumpet for it is this angel who is due to sound the Final Trumpet announcing the End of Time and heralding the Last Judgment.

Islam also honors Gabriel (*Jibril* in Arabic) as the great Messenger of the Lord. It was he who

Left: Lilies are a symbol of the Archangel Gabriel, seen here in feminine form.

was sent to dictate the *Koran* to Mohammed, an illiterate Arab merchant, having appeared in a brilliant white light asking "Sleeper, how long will you sleep?" Mohammed's followers know *Jibril* as the Angel of Truth, and it was he who finally bore the Prophet to Paradise.

Associations and Symbolism

In ancient Judaic lore the Archangel Gabriel was considered to be female, indeed the only female angel in the Heavenly Hierarchies. We know, of course, that angels have no gender in a reproductive sense, but in an energetic sense many tend to one polarity or the other. Gabriel certainly tends towards the feminine polarity, as many of his attributes bear out.

Above: The Archangel Gabriel, as messenger of the Lord, delivers a message to John the Baptist.

   Gabriel stands in the West, which is associated with the feminine element, Water. As a planetary angel, Gabriel is the ruler of Monday, the day of the Moon and the sign of Cancer, whose ruling planet is the Moon. The Moon, as consort of the Sun, is the most feminine of heavenly bodies. Her cycles govern the menstrual cycle in women, the ocean tides, and the pulses of vital energy that course around the Earth. The thirteenth-century Sufi poet Ruzbihan Baqli describes a vision in which

"In the first rank I saw Gabriel, like a maiden, or like the Moon among the stars ... he is the most beautiful of Angels."

   Gabriel's colors are those of the Moon: silver and shining white. He is best petitioned around the time of the New or Full Moon, but you can reflect on his love, power, and beauty every time you look at the Moon.

The Archangel Raphael

Divine Physician and Merry Companion

The Angel of Healing and of Science and Knowledge, the Archangel Raphael is one of only three angels named in the Bible, the others being fellow Archangels Michael and Gabriel. Raphael first appears in the Apocryphal *Book of Tobit*, where, disguised as a fellow traveler, he shows Tobias how to use and prepare various parts of a great fish to help rid him of the demon Asmodeus. He then shows him how to use the fish's gallbladder to restore his father Tobit's eyesight. The story is the best scriptural example of Raphael as a teacher of the healing arts. Another famous story of Raphael tells of how God sent him with a ring to assist King Solomon in the building of the Temple. The ring's seal was a pentagram with the power to bind demons. Known as "The Seal of Solomon," it is one of the most important tools of ceremonial magic and forms the basis for the important angel invocation known as the Ritual of the Pentagram (see page 110). The pentagram is one of the oldest medical symbols and pharmacists in Europe were still using it as a trademark until recent times.

Above: The Archangel Raphael tells Tobias how to make medicine from a fish in a scene from the *Book of Tobit*.

Associations and Symbolism

Raphael stands in the East and rules the Element of Air. His day is Wednesday, the day of Mercury (*mercredi* in French) and he is closely connected with the planet Mercury, once embodied by the Greek/Roman god Hermes/Mercury.

The Egyptian Hermes, Hermes Trismegistus or Thoth, brought to mankind such sacred arts as geometry and alchemy. The correct use of these "Hermetic" arts is to heal the rift between humanity and Heaven. This transformation was the goal of the alchemists who petitioned Mercurius, as they called him, to assist them. The name *Raphael* means "The Shining One Who Heals" and Raphael, like Mercurius, helps us to heal ourselves and shows us that we can use knowledge to reach the Kingdom of Heaven. He also has a great sense of humor and is an amusing guide and companion on the journey of life. As such he is often depicted dressed as a pilgrim wearing a hat, holding a caduceus staff in one hand and a vial of medicine in the other. Raphael is designated Chief of the Virtues and is said to have wings at his temples, his shoulders and, like Hermes/Mercury, at his ankles. His colors are those of the dawn: yellow, orange, and pale blue.

Above: The Greek god Hermes, seen here with his caduceus wand, is associated with the Archangel Raphael.

The Archangel Uriel
Fire of God and Angel of the Cataclysm

U riel is one of the most powerful and formidable of the angelic hosts. As an Angel of the Presence, he is able to reflect the unimaginable brightness of the Throne. His glyph is a lightning flash, and it was he, as Angel of the Cataclysm, who was sent to warn Noah of the impending deluge. In Milton's *Paradise Lost* he is described as the most eagle-eyed of all the angels. Nevertheless, he fails to see through the disguise of Satan, who tricks him into giving him directions to Earth and then to the Garden of Eden. Apart from this one slip, Uriel has a reputation of invincible power and authority. In the *Sibylline Oracles*, it is he who holds the keys to Hell and is due to tear down its gates on Judgment

Day. He can be a terrifying Angel of Retribution who punishes sinners, but he is also a dependable guide to humanity and an interpreter of Divine Truth. In the Apoycryphal *Second Book of Esdras*, he teaches the prophet the great lesson of humility by shaming him for presuming to judge the ways of God.

Left: Archangel Uriel, Angel of the Cataclysm. The scroll and lightning are two of his symbols.

Noe fintne. rpa hine nergcbo hehc· hynbe þam hal
gan· hæþon cynunge· ongan· oþoyt lice þ hof pyrcan·
micle mıhe ciſtre· magum rægbe· þþæt þrſulıe þing·
þæbuum torfunð· næbe pıcc· hıe· neþoheon þæy· ge
ræıh þa ymb pıncıa popır· þæn fæye mæoð· gæþon
hıpa mærce· gæhro hlıpıgdan· ınnan ȝutan· ðonðan
líme· gepæprınoð pıð flode· þrıí noth· þy relðcun·
þıy ryndrıg cynn· Symle bıð þy hkandna· þehıc hınðoh
pæþı· rpæınce ræ rencdamar· rpıðon bkacuð·

Associations and Symbolism

As Angel of the North, Uriel rules the element of Earth and the season of winter. His planet is Uranus, and he shares that planet's affinity with electricity and suddenness of action. He can provide flashes of inspiration and insight. He is the Angel of the Eleventh Hour, who can be called upon to intervene in moments of extreme crisis. He rules Saturday (with Cassiel) and the Sign of Aquarius. White quartz crystals, as "frozen light" and transmitters of electrical energy, are sacred to him. He is sometimes depicted holding a book and scroll, symbolizing God's Law. As St. Uriel, his symbol is an open palm bearing a flame. Uriel's other titles include Angel of Prophecy, Angel of Repentance, Angel of Thunder and Lightning, Angel of Terror, Light of God, and Angel of the Kabbalah. He can be envisaged as a huge figure of incredible brightness surrounded by a rainbow corona with lightning flashing from a crown of quartz. His face is set firm and his electric blue eyes penetrate all.

The Planetary Angels

∞

In twelfth- and thirteenth-century Moorish Spain there was a great flourishing of esoteric philosophy inspired by the cultural cross-fertilization of Arab, Jewish, and Christian traditions. Christian scholars discovered the literary treasures of Greece and Alexandrian Egypt, translating them from Arabic into Latin, bringing Europe out of the Dark Ages to the threshold of the Renaissance. It was also here that the classic *Kabbalah* text, the *Zohar*, was written. The correspondences found between the different strains of astrology, alchemy, religion, magic, and mysticism started a rich synthesizing process that continues to this day.

It is also from the Spain of this period that we have the first documentary example connecting certain angels with the planets. The connecting of the seven classical planets, which include the Sun and Moon, with the days of the week goes back at least as far as the Romans. The planets are seen as archetypal energetic beings. The weaving interplay between them as they spin though their orbits characterizes every moment and affects everything on Earth. The planetary angels can be understood as the "intelligences" of the planets, reflecting their most positive aspects. They inspire us to live in harmony with the spheres, and assist us in the specific areas that are their domain.

Invoking the Planetary Angels

To petition a planetary angel, write your wish in the form of a prayer using angelic script (for a full explanation of this see page 116). To invoke a planetary angel you will need a piece of cloth, preferably silk, in the color of the planetary angel you wish to invoke. This is placed in the center of the room you use to perform the ritual. Stand on this while reciting the prayer of invocation. You may place objects sacred to the planetary angel, as listed in the table of correspondences, around the edge of the cloth to help tune in the energies. Candles corresponding in color and number to the planetary angel in question should be lit, along with some corresponding incense. Saltwater may be sprinkled around the edges of the room to purify it and keep unwelcome influences away. When all is prepared, begin the invocation, facing east. Here is an example of an invocation, which can be adapted to any of the planetary angels:

In the name of the Almighty, Creator of all that is, I call upon you great Angel ...., as ruler of this day and Prince of the planet ...., to grant this my wish, Whose concern comes under your special influence. Please...................(state wish). May this wish be realized for the good of myself and to the harm of none.

Now turn to the south and repeat the invocation, and again to the west and north. Then turn once more to the east and, spreading wide your arms, say:

I honor and thank you Angel .... for granting this, my wish, in the name of the Almighty. hail and farewell.

Make a bow and repeat to the other three directions.

Michael
Ruler of the Sun

As regent of Sunday, Michael, in his role as planetary angel, assumes the characteristics of the Sun, mitigating any tendency to excess and encouraging its virtues. Michael's name means "He Who Is As God," which is fitting as the Sun is the cosmic symbol of the Almighty, being the great light of the world sustaining all life through the radiation of light and warmth. The Sun represents abundance, vitality, energy, and power. It also stands for material and spiritual growth and perfection, sharing its symbol with gold, the metal it evolves to perfection in the crucible of the Earth.

The Sun's influence is benign, but too much can be spoiling. With Michael's help we can ensure against pride, selfishness, and egocentricity, receiving instead the illumination to awe us into humility and lead us into grace. Then can we reflect the light of love and share it with our neighbors.

Noon on Sundays, especially during summer, is the best time to invoke or petition Michael. Look out for omens involving his correspondences during the following week. Results may be as long as a year in coming, but will often unfold by the following solstice.

Below: Orange and yellow butterflies are sacred to Michael as planetary ruler of the Sun.

Correspondences of Michael

Element: *Fire*
Metal: *Gold*
Number: *6*
Choir: *Powers*
Sephirah: *Tiphareth*
Deities: *Apollo, Helios, Bel, Ra, Mithras*
Colors: *Yellow, gold*
Animals: *Lion, all cats*
Bird: *Blackbird*
Insects: *Yellow and orange butterflies, daddy longlegs*
Stones: *Ruby, tiger's eye, amber, chrysolite*
Spices: *Cinnamon, cloves, white and black pepper, ginger, saffron*
Incense: *Frankincense, myrrh, copal, cinnamon, bergamot*
Flowers: *Peony, marigold, sunflower, passion flower, cyclamen*
Trees: *Walnut, ash, citrus trees, laurel, juniper*
Foods: *Grapes, rice, strawberries, olives, almonds*
healing plants: *Melissa, chamomile, eyebright, St. John's Wort, rosemary, mistletoe*
Body parts: *Heart, spine, solar plexus, eyes*
Body functions: *Circulation, heat and energy distribution*
Virtues: *Health, vitality, organization, power*
Professions: *Leading personalities in all professions*
Activities: *All creative activities*
Keyword: *Vitality*

Above: Michael leads the angels of light in the battle against the angels of darkness.

43

Gabriel
Lord of the Moon

Gabriel is Lord of the Moon, ruling Monday and the sign of Cancer. For us the Moon is the most significant heavenly body after the Sun. There is an old Islamic legend that the Moon was once as bright as the Sun, so that the creatures of Earth could not distinguish day from night. Allah therefore commanded *Jibril* (Gabriel) to soften the light of the Moon. The angel brushed it with his wings, transmuting it from fiery gold to cool silver. Gabriel, therefore, represents the light, the conscious intelligence of the Moon, while mitigating the effects of its dark, unconscious side.

Everything that grows upon the Earth does so in rhythm with the Moon, which rules all bodily fluids. As the *Bhagavad-Gita* says, "By becoming the Moon full of juices, I nourish all plants." The Moon is motherly, nurturing, sustaining growth. It rules dreams, the emotions, sensuality, intuition, the way we feel. Its dark side is the unconscious, the wilder, baser instincts. Gabriel can help control "full-moon fever," softening any lycanthropic tendencies (the power to transform oneself into a wolf). His influence soothes the spirit and nurtures the soul.

Gabriel is best contacted on a Monday. Letters of petition should be written in silver or violet ink on white paper using Theban script (see page 117). To perform a ritual invocation (see page 41) you should burn silver candles and stand on a square of white or violet silk. Look out for any of Gabriel's correspondences coming into your waking life or dreams as a sign of consent. These should appear within 28 days, a lunar month, often before the next New Moon.

Left: White lilies are a sacred symbol of the Archangel Gabriel and are governed by the Moon.

44

Correspondences of Gabriel

Element: *Water*
Metal: *Silver*
Number: *9*
Choir: *Cherubim*
Sephirah: *Yesod*
Deities: *Isis, Artemis, Diana, Selene, Cybele, Arianrhod, Astarte*
Colors: *Silver, violet*
Animals: *Shellfish, wolf*
Birds: *Owl, nightingale*
Insects: *Moths, spiders*
Stones: *Moonstone, pearls*
Spices: *Turmeric, nutmeg*
Incense: *Camphor, jasmine, ylang-ylang*
Flowers: *White lilies, acanthus, water lilies, pale iris*
Trees: *Willows, magnolia*
Foods: *Papaya, pumpkin, water melon*
Healing plants: *Chaste tree, cleavers, opium poppy, periwinkle*
Body parts: *Brain, womb, bladder, stomach, pancreas*
Body functions: *Menstruation, growth, fertility, glandular secretion*
Virtues: *Sensitivity, motherliness, benevolence*
Professions: *Midwife, doctor, nurse, teacher, nanny, gynecologist*
Activities: *All water sports, dowsing, meditation, fasting*
Keyword: *Feeling*

Above: The Annunciation is depicted in Mary's words to the Archangel Gabriel, "Let it be with me according to your word."

Raphael

Angel of Mercury

As a planetary angel, Raphael is the regent of Wednesday and embodies the qualities of its ruling planet Mercury. Personified by the Greeks and Romans as Hermes/Mercurius, the messenger of the gods, he was often depicted as an androgynous youth wearing winged sandals and a winged cap. These are the clues to Mercury's main attributes—swiftness and mental processes. Mercury governs travel, communications, language, writing, and the intellect. It has an ambivalent, unreliable quality akin to the trickster figures in some traditions, who set pitfalls for people to show them their foolishness.

Raphael, however, can be depended on not to see you wrong. He is the Quicksilver Messenger mediating between Heaven and Earth. He can help us improve our judgment and ability to communicate, and achieve greater mental power. If we need help adapting to changes in circumstance, Raphael can be called upon. His is the intelligence behind telecommunications and computers, and he can even help you avoid disastrous computer viruses.

Raphael's planetary colors are orange and yellow. His response to petitions and invocations is likely to be very swift. You can expect to see omens of consent within seven days and results just as quickly. Likely omens include unexpected letters and practical jokes. You can visualize Raphael with additional wings at temples and ankles, and holding a caduceus staff. His aura is yellow-gold and he oscillates extremely rapidly.

Left: The planet Mercury lies closest to the Sun, which it orbits in about 180 days.

Correspondences of Raphael

Element: *Air*
Metal: *Quicksilver*
Number: *8*
Choir: *Virtues*
Sephirah: *Hod*
Deities: *Hermes, Mercury, Thoth, Quetzalcoatl,*
Viracocha, Kukulkan
Colors: *Orange, yellow*
Animals: *Coyote, monkeys*
Birds: *Ibis, raven, corvids, most other birds*
Insects: *Flies*
Stones: *Opals, topaz, tourmaline, carnelian, peridot*
Spices: *Caraway, aniseed, cubeb pepper*
Incense: *Anise, lavender, gum arabic, storax*
Flowers: *Azaleas, red foxglove, lily of the valley,*
elecampane
Trees: *Hazel, acacia, myrtle, mulberry*
Foods: *Celery, oats, endive, carrot, licorice, parsnip, pomegranate*
healing plants: *Wormwood, digitalis, mandrake, valerian, skullcap, parsley*
Body parts: *Ears, tongue, nervous system, hands, feet, lungs, spinal cord, thyroid*
Body functions: *Mental and nervous processes, hearing, speech, respiration,*
coordination
Virtues: *Communication, mediation, trickery*
Professions: *Writer, agent, the media,*
computer programmer, interpreter, diplomat,
healer
Activities: *Buying and selling, collecting,*
social clubs, letter writing
Keyword: *Speed*

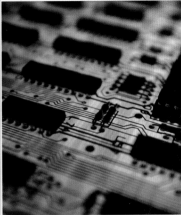

Above: Raphael rules all
information and communication
processes and systems.

Right: All monkeys are sacred to
Raphael in his role as planetary
ruler of Mercury.

Hagiel
Ruler of Venus

hagiel is regent of Venus and of Friday. He is a chief of two choirs—Virtues and Principalities—and is listed by some authorities as one of the Great Archangels. His name translates as "Grace of God" and he is believed to have been one of the few angels given the honor of assisting at Creation. Tradition names him as the angel who bore the prophet Enoch to Heaven.

It is said that merely pronouncing Hagiel's name can provide protection from malign influences. As ruler of the zodiacal sign of Libra, Hagiel helps mediate between opposites and integrate diverse elements into harmonious balance. As the Angel of Venus, Hagiel creates beauty, love, affection, and harmony. He can intercede in all kinds of relationships—family, friends, lovers—to end quarrels, heal rifts, forge friendships, and bring lovers together.

It is in this last regard that he is most commonly petitioned. He will not help someone win the love of another against their will, but he can create the most favorable opportunities for a relationship to flourish.

To write a letter of petition to Hagiel, you can use pink or green ink on white, pink, or green paper. The letter should be written in Theban script (see page 116) and read aloud on a Friday night at around 10 o'clock, preferably during the waxing Moon. Then place the letter in an envelope with a petal from one of his

Left: Aphrodite, the Greek goddess of love. She and her Roman equivalent, Venus, correspond to the Angel Hagiel.

sacred flowers, or a pinch of his favorite herbs or spices. After 28 days the envelope and its contents should be burned. During this period, be on the lookout for signs that your wish has received consent. Any of Hagiel's correspondences making a welcome or unmissable appearance in your life can be construed as a good sign that your wish will be fulfilled.

Correspondences of Hagiel

Element: *Air*
Metal: *Copper*
Number: 7
Choirs: *Virtues, Principalities*
Sephirah: *Netzach*
Deities: *Aphrodite, Sukra, Ishtar, Benten, Lakshmi, Chenrezi*
Colors: *Pink (Libran), green (Taurean)*
Animals: *Deer, rabbits*
Birds: *Doves, swallows*
Insects: *Butterflies*
Stones: *Emerald, rose quartz, opal, jade, malachite, pink coral*
Spices: *Coriander, cinnamon, pink peppercorns, thyme*
Incense: *Sandalwood, storax, galbanum, valerian, violet*
Flowers: *Red/pink roses, orchids, primrose, violet, columbine*
Trees: *Apple, pear, cherry, elder, linden, chestnut*
Foods: *Strawberry, blackberry, peach*
Healing plants: *Yarrow, lady's mantle, motherwort, vervain, wormwood*
Body parts: *Complexion, upper lip, throat, breasts, kidneys, inner sexual organs*
Body functions: *Cell and nerve formation, diuretic and emetic processes, sense of smell*
Virtues: *Harmony, proportion, beauty, affection*
Professions: *Musicians, actors, diplomats, entertainers, hairdressers, designers*
Activities: *Weddings, parties, cozy relaxation, love affairs*
Keyword: *Grace*

Above: Angel musicians are a common feature of Renaissance art. Music is closely associated with Hagiel.

Camael

Angel of Mars

Camael is the regent of Tuesday. As ruler of Mars, the planet of fiery passion and war, he has an ambivalent role in angel lore with both dark and light characteristics ascribed to him. As Samael, he has even been equated with Satan, while Enoch describes him as one of God's favorite angels. This conflicting picture is reflected by the traditional astrological image of Mars as a malign body at conflict with the other planets. The negative aspects of Mars include ruthlessness, destruction, and brutality. Its positive aspects are determination and willpower, the courage and passion necessary to survive and flourish in the flux of chaos.

As individuals we are engaged in a struggle for self-determination. The self-assertion this requires can create conflict. Camael teaches us how to cope with conflict, helping to transmute competitive aggression into gentle cooperation. He can also provide us with strength and fortitude when we are the victims of aggression. He will not help us slay our enemies, but he can help protect us from them and show us the lessons they teach us. Camael is a great guide and protector. He provides us with the courage and determination to overcome all the obstacles that we have set in our paths.

Camael can be visualized as a great figure in red, emitting green sparks. His symbol is an upright sword. He should be petitioned or invoked on a Tuesday (see page 41).

Camael responds swiftly and petitions should be burned within seven days. During this period look out for signs of consent. Even slightly alarming experiences involving his correspondences, such as fire and steel knives, may be a positive sign.

Correspondences of Camael

Element: *Fire*
Metal: *Iron*
Number: *5*
Choir: *Seraphim*
Sephirah: *Geburah*
Deities: *Ares, Tiu / Tyr, Bishamon, all war gods*
Colors: *Red*
Animals: *Fox, ram*
Birds: *Robin, sparrow*
Insects: *Scorpion, all stinging insects apart from bees*
Stones: *Ruby, garnet, bloodstone, carnelian, red coral*
Spices: *All peppers, chilies, cumin, mustard*
Incense: *Cyprus, aloes, tobacco, pine, red cedar*
Flowers: *Anemones, geranium, madder, yellow gentian, honeysuckle*
Trees: *Thorn trees, pines, savin, cypress, rhododendron*
Foods: *Pineapple, onion, garlic, horseradish, Chinese rhubarb*
healing plants: *Hawthorn, nettle, sarsaparilla, vomic nut, basil*
Body parts: *Muscular system, red corpuscles, sex organs, gall, astral body*
Body functions: *Body heat, kundalini, blood formation*
Virtues: *Courage, determination, passion, protection*
Professions: *Armed forces, firefighting, mechanics, athletes, technicians, surgeons*
Activities: *Competitive games, martial arts, drumming, crafts*
Keyword: *Martial*

Below: Mars is the planet of fire and conflict, destructive elements that are mitigated and balanced by Camael.

Zadkiel

Ruler of Jupiter

Zadkiel is regent of Jupiter and of Thursday. He is often named as chief of the Fifth Heaven and the Choir of Dominions. According to Jewish lore he was the angel who stayed the hand of Abraham on Mount Moriah as he was about to sacrifice his son Isaac. He is one of the two chief generals of the Archangel Michael, joining him in the heat of battle with the infernal hosts. As the ruler of Jupiter, he is accorded all the attributes and correspondences of that planet. Zadkiel is a benevolent and jovial angel of mercy. A generous celestial banker ruling all matters of prosperity, speculation, wages, and debts, he can solve problems with banks and creditors, and will assist in efforts to earn money as long as the ambition and nature of the work is "clean." Zadkiel helps reconcile mundane law with Divine Justice, and is the patron of lawyers and judges. He is visualized as a kingly figure wearing violet and purple with an aura or wings of radiant royal blue. A letter of petition to Zadkiel should be written in Theban script (see page 116). It can be written in blue or purple ink, on white or blue paper or parchment.

Right: Zadkiel staying the hand of Abraham on Mount Moriah.

To perform a ritual invocation (see page 41) you should light a blue or purple candle, burn one of Zadkiel's preferred incenses, and decorate your altar with corresponding flowers or objects. Perform your invocation while standing on a square of blue or purple silk. If any of these correspondences should catch your eye or appear unexpectedly in the days or weeks following your petition or invocation, you may take it as a sign that your wish has been heard.

Correspondences of Zadkiel

Element: *Fire*
Metal: *Tin*
Number: *4*
Choir: *Dominions*
Sephirah: *Chesed*
Deities: *Zeus/Jupiter/Jove, Sobek, Math, Dagda*
Colors: *Mauve, blue, purple*
Animals: *Whale, elephant*
Birds: *Swan, duck*
Insects: *Bee*
Stones: *Sapphire, lapis lazuli, amethyst, turquoise, tanzanite*
Spices: *Fennel, nutmeg*
Incense: *Myrrh, sandalwood, benzoin, gum mastic, cedar*
Flowers: *Lilac, carnations, hyacinth*
Trees: *Oak, ash, cedar*
Foods: *Apricot, tomato, fig*

Healing plants: *Arnica, borage, lemon balm, sage, ginseng, comfrey*
Body parts: *Liver, arteries, digestive organs, buttocks, right ear, feet*
Body functions: *Immune system, energy conservation*
Virtues: *Generosity, fairness, benevolence, mercy*
Professions: *Financial, legal, fishermen, sailors,*
Activities: *Gambling, horse racing, fishing, archery*
Keyword: *Jovial*

53

Cassiel

Regent of Saturn

Cassiel is the ruler of Saturday and Saturn, the planet of restriction and inhibition. The most distant and slowest moving of the visible planets, Saturn is where the descent into matter begins. On the Path of Return he is the Guardian of the Threshold, restricting entry into the heavenly realms to the most worthy. In mythology Saturn is characterized as Old Father Time with a scythe and hourglass, which led to an association with death. Saturn is a hard taskmaster—strict, demanding, and unforgiving of the frivolous. Bad reactions to the influence of Saturn can lead to isolation and inhibition. As the intelligence of Saturn, Cassiel is therefore known as the Angel of Tears. He is not, however, a punishing angel. He is here to help, but the lessons he has to teach us are the hard facts of life.

Cassiel's challenge is "How much do you care?" If your answer is "Enough to make the necessary effort," then we have won ourselves a powerful ally. Cassiel can transmute self-pity into humility, escapism into responsibility, listlessness into purpose. Letters of petition to Cassiel should be written on Saturdays. For invocations, use purple candles and silk. Saturn being slow-moving, Cassiel may take a long time to respond, and omens may not appear for several months. If a quick solution is sought, the Quicksilver Messenger Raphael can be asked to intercede with Cassiel on our behalf. This should be done during Raphael's hour on Saturday nights at 10 o'clock.

Left: Saturnus, the Roman god of the planet Saturn, is depicted here with wings like Cassiel, planetary ruler of Saturn.

Correspondences of Cassiel

Element: Earth
Metal: Lead
Number: 3
Choir: Powers
Sephirah: Binah
Deities: Cronus, Ceridwen
Colors: Iridescent black, purple
Animals: Tortoise, beaver, sloth, vole, worm
Birds: Crow, rook, heron
Insects: Centipede, termite, all building and slow-moving insects
Stones: Onyx, jet, diamond, obsidian, black corals, coal
Spice: Fenugreek
Incense: Myrrh, spikenard, harmal, copal, aloes
Flowers: Most irises, cornflower, pansy, verbascum
Trees: Beech, holly, poplar, Scotch pine, yew

Above: As planetary angel of Saturn, Cassiel rules all hardening processes, including the formation of rocks and bones.

Foods: Maize, barley, rye, tamarind, beets, quince
Healing plants: Equisetum, aconite, belladonna, cannabis, red root, uva ursi
Body parts: Bone structure, teeth, tendons, joints
Body functions: All hardening and aging processes, blood circulation in tissues
Virtues: Discipline, humility, perseverance, acceptance, wisdom
Professions: Real estate, education, mining, construction, archaeology, dentistry
Activities: Mountaineering, carving, crafts, collecting, study, distance running
Keyword: Saturnine

The Outer Planets

The three "invisible" planets of the solar system, which cannot be seen in the night sky by the naked eye, were discovered in comparatively recent times. They have been incorporated into modern astrology and they also have their ruling angels, although only Uriel, as Angel of Uranus, can be directly invoked. The planets of Neptune and Pluto are deemed in angelology to be so subtle in their effects that they are beyond the sphere of tangible influence on individual humans.

Neptune–Asariel

Asariel rules Neptune and, with Zadkiel, Thursday and the sign of Pisces. He influences the faculties of intuition and imagination and is strongly connected with mysticism. He mitigates the less positive Neptunian responses such as deception and delusion.

Pluto–Azrael

Azrael is the regent of Pluto, ruling Tuesday and Scorpio with Camael. Pluto is the planet of providence and Azrael works unceasingly to help the transformation of humanity as a whole. He contends with such dangerous responses to the energy of Pluto as fanaticism and totalitarianism.

Uranus–Uriel

As the planetary angel of Uranus, Uriel rules Saturday and the sign of Aquarius with Cassiel. He represents freedom, independence, and new ideas. Uranus is the planet most closely connected to electricity, and can bring about sudden change and flashes of enlightenment. Uriel can mitigate the trickier aspects of Uranus, such as impulsiveness, obstinacy, an inability to adapt, and nervous tension.

Angels of the Zodiac

The planetary angels also govern the various signs of the Zodiac. This concurs
with traditional modern astrology, where the planets also rule particular signs.

Aries	Camael
Taurus	Hagiel
Gemini	Raphael
Cancer	Gabriel
Leo	Michael
Virgo	Raphael
Libra	Hagiel
Scorpio	Azrael and Camael
Saggitarius	Zadkiel
Capricorn	Cassiel
Aquarius	Uriel and Cassiel
Pisces	Asariel and Zadkiel

The Guardian Angels

❧

The idea that people have guardian angels, or spirits that are appointed to protect them, is as old as human culture. In ancient Mesopotamia, the cradle of Middle Eastern civilization, these protective beings were considered personal gods, known as "massar sulmi." This tradition was adopted by later civilizations in the region, such as the Babylonians and Chaldeans, who in turn were to influence Judaism, and hence Christianity and Islam.

The idea of a personal guardian spirit can be traced to cultures past and present throughout the rest of the world as well. In Japan this spirit is a *kami*; in Burma, a *nat*; and in ancient Greece its equivalent was a *daemon*. In pre-Christian Rome the *genius* and *juno* protected boys and girls respectively. Native Americans and all shamanistic cultures believe in spirit guides that manifest in any form, particularly as totem animals or ancestor spirits. In Islam, each person has two pairs of *hafaza*, one for the day and one for the night. These guardian angels protect the faithful from the demonic *jinn* and record the person's every act in a book to be presented at Judgment Day. The *Koran* states: "He [Allah] sends forth guardians who watch over you and carry away your souls without fail when death overtakes you."

In Jewish tradition everyone has a guardian angel assigned to them at birth. The *Talmud* states that each person has no fewer than 11,000 guardian angels, although a more prevalent belief is that there are two personal angels per person, one good, the other bad. This view is shared by the Catholic Church, a tradition dating back at least as far as the third century C.E.

Guardian angels are not officially part of Catholic dogma, despite Jesus's saying, of children, that "in heaven their angels do always behold the face of my Father which is in heaven" (*Mathew 18:10*). Nevertheless, Catholic children are traditionally taught to recite a prayer to their guardian angel, to which Pope John XXIII referred on the

Above: Small children who appear to be inventing imaginary or invisible friends may, in reality, be communicating with their guardian angels.

Feast of the Guardian Angels, October 2, 1959: "We must have a lively and profound devotion to our own Guardian Angel, and should often and trustfully repeat the dear prayer we were taught in the days of our childhood." In English this prayer is as follows:

"Angel of God who are my guardian,
Enlighten, watch over, support and rule me,
Who was entrusted to you by the heavenly piety. Amen."

Catholics also believe in "tutelary" angels, who protect all places, from nations to the smallest communities, as well as families, altars, and churches. All guardian and tutelary angels are in the lowest angelic hierarchy, the Choir of Angels.

In the view of Rudolf Steiner, the twentieth-century Austrian philosopher, our guardian angel has been with us throughout all our incarnations and knows the entire history of our soul. It is the inner teacher, the "still small voice inside."

But how do we recognize it? How can we communicate with it? The first thing to do is to acknowledge its existence, not just as a possibility, but as a reality, however we choose to define that reality—psychic phenomenon, for example, or God-created spirit. The definition is not important; in fact it can be a good start to acknowledge our ignorance. Like all of Creation, this is a great mystery. But this time it's personal, deeply personal. This is an entity that knows us better than we know ourselves. That can be quite humbling, even alarming. If we are alarmed it is an indication that we have not yet reconciled ourselves to all of our doings.

But nothing can be hidden. A recapitulation of our lives—all of our actions and experiences—is a very good preparation for meeting the guardian angel. This process can generate every kind of emotion, but, if we are able to let everything go, including self-pity, anger, hurt, and guilt, and accept responsibility for our story, then we can reach that very special, precious state where the true self resides: humility. This is where many of us first encounter, heart to heart, that endlessly patient, compassionate presence that knows us so well, the Holy Guardian Angel.

Discovering your guardian angel's name

Some people find that it helps them to communicate with their guardian angel, or to connect with it for the first time, if they know its name, for traditionally all angels have names. There are various ways of doing this, all of which involve a period of purification of at least 24 hours. During this time there should be no sexual activity and minimal intake of addictive and stimulating substances. Meat is best avoided as are spicy foods which can be stimulating. The idea is to calm the whole nervous and energetic system. This way we can be at our most receptive and intuitive.

The most straightforward way of divining your guardian angel's name is to write every consonant in the alphabet on a little square of card—if you have a Scrabble set, the letters are ideal—and put them all in a bag. Light a white candle and burn some incense, ideally frankincense or copal and myrrh. Now, after pausing to center yourself, state your intention with an invocation along these lines:

Dear Divine Angel
Who has always been
My protector, guide, and ally,
Please guide my hand to draw the
    letters
That spell your holy name,
So that I may write it upon my
    heart
And honor you as the friend thou art.
When I call your name please be
    with me
And show me so I can clearly see
The path of light and of love.

Below: Many Christians believe that the guardian angels carry our souls to heaven after death.

Above: You can write the consonants of the alphabet on little squares of card or paint them on to pebbles or beads before placing them in a bag.

Now take a letter from the bag and write it down on a blank piece of paper. Return the letter to the bag, shake the letters around, and take out another. Repeat this process until you have written down three or four letters—let your intuition guide you as to how many.

Say you have drawn out the three letters M, D, and R, you then flesh out the name with the vowels of your choice adding the letters EL at the end. You might then come up with "aMaDRiEL" or "oMDiRiEL". Try out different combinations, always keeping the original consonants in the same order. You are bound to come up with a name that sounds right. This will be the name of your guardian angel.

Don't worry if this seems an irrational or arbitrary method. You are allowing the Universe, or rather your guardian angel, to guide you in a very straightforward way. Trust the process.

Patron Angels

There are many angels who rule over elements of nature, such as rain and wind or certain attributes, such as strength or wisdom. These angels are called patron angels and you can find some of the best-known ones here.

Agriculture–*Risnuch, Habuhiah*
Air–*Raphael*
Animals, tame–*Behemiel*
Animals, wild–*Thuriel*
Aspirations–*Gabriel*
Autumn/Fall–*Guabarel*
Birds–*Arael, Anpiel*
Chance–*Barakiel, Rubiel*
Childbirth–*Armisael, Gabriel*
Compassion–*Rahmiel*
Conception–*Lailah*
Dawn–*Raphael*
Daylight–*Shamshiel*
Death–*Tzaphkiel, Gabriel*
Destiny–*Oriel*
Dreams–*Gabriel*
Earth–*Uriel*
Eyesight–*Mahzian*
Fertility–*Samandiriel*
Fidelity–*Tezalel*
Fire–*Michael*
Forests–*Zuphlas*
Freedom–*Terathel*
Friendship–*Mihr*
Good health–*Rehael*
harmony–*Itqal*
healing–*Raphael*
hope–*Phanuel*
Justice–*Zadkiel, Vasiariah*
Knowledge–*Raphael*
Lost objects–*Rochel*

Marriage–*Anael/Hagiel*
Memory–*Zachariel*
Mercy–*Vasiariah, Zadkiel*
Night–*Lailah*
Nourishment–*Asda*
Passion–*Jelial*
Patience–*Achaiah*
Peace–*Seraphiel*
Plants–*Sachluph*
Pregnancy–*Temeluch*
Prosperity–*Librabis*
Protection–*Lahabiel*
Purity–*Tahariel*
Rain–*Riddia, Matariel, Zafiel*
Science–*Raphael*
Sea–*Rahab*
Snow–*Shalgiel*
Solitude–*Cassiel*
Song–*Radueriel*
Streams–*Nahariel*
Strength–*Zaruch*
Summer–*Gargatel*
Thunder–*Ramiel, Uriel*
Travel–*Raphael*
Trees–*Maktiel*
Truth–*Amitiel*
Twilight–*Aftiel*
Water–*Gabriel*
Wilderness–*Oriphiel*
Wind–*Moriah*
Womb–*Armisael*

The
ASSISTING
ANGELS

Angels sustain everything in the manifest Universe. With their special mission to support and protect humanity there are angels responsible for every archetypal human situation. In the following pages we will meet some of the best-known angels who have been helping us for millennia. The invocations and rituals provided should be understood as guidelines. Always feel free to address the angels in your own way. An honest and open heart is the only compulsory part of any ritual.

Angels of Love

All angels are essentially angels of love, reflecting as
they do the light of the Almighty, which is love, and
working unceasingly for the harmonious unfolding of
the Universe. Of all the angels, though, Archangel
hagiel, the planetary ruler of Venus, is the principle
Angel of Love, particularly
concerning human
relationships, working
for harmony, love,
and affection among
people. he has many
angels who work
with him, some of
whom are responsible
for particular aspects
of love and relationships.

Marriage
Anael

Anael is another name for the Archangel Hagiel, ruler of Venus, the planet of love. Anael is the Angel of Marriage, blessing couples who choose to sanctify their love by splicing their destinies as husband and wife. Anael delights in all love and affection expressed between people, but the faith and commitment required by marriage receive his special blessings when he is invited to grant them. If you hope for marriage as the fulfillment of a relationship in which you or people you care for are already involved, you can call upon Anael for assistance. Anael cannot interfere in people's destinies, but, if it is possible for your wish to come true, you can be sure that Anael will help open all the necessary doors that lead to wedlock. Here is a ritual to invoke Anael's aid.

Remove the thorns from a single red rose and a single white rose. Hold the stems together and slip over them three rings—one silver, one gold, and one copper. Place them on your altar or on your bed with a white candle on either side. Light the candles and burn some sandalwood or storax. Face the east and recite this prayer or something similar in your own words:

In the name of the Almighty Creator,
In whom all things have their beginning and end,
I invoke you, Archangel Anael,
Ordained as the Angel of marriage,
To bless and nurture the relationship between .... and
.... (fill in names),
Allowing it to blossom into the true devotion,
Made sacred by holy matrimony.
I thank and honor you for hearing this,
my wish,
In the name of the Almighty.

Harmony

Itqal

Itqal is one of the angels of the sphere of Venus and Libra working with Archangel Hagiel. He is traditionally invoked to help heal rifts and resolve quarrels. The people closest to us are often the ones we find ourselves in conflict with, especially close relatives. This is because we can't help getting under each other's skin. When this leads to serious quarrels we often forget or even deny how much we really love each other.

Itqal can help dissolve these conflicts and restore harmony. This does not mean that we stop expressing how we really feel, because this is vital to greater understanding. Rather we are reminded that kindness and consideration are always more helpful than anger and blame. Itqal can be invoked at any time, but for more chronic problems Fridays are best. Six candles may be lit, six being the number of harmony. Sandalwood is the best incense to burn:

In the name of the loving Creator,
From whom all perfection springs,
I call upon you, sweet Angel Itqal,
As Prince of harmony and Peace,
To dissolve the conflicts that
    separate us.
May we find love and
    understanding
To replace hurt and antagonism.
I thank and honor you for hearing
    this prayer
In the name of the Almighty.

Passion
Jelial

J elial is said to be a Seraph whose name is inscribed on the Tree of Life. The Seraphim are the very highest of the angelic choirs, burning with the reflected glory of God, and do not normally associate themselves with such base creatures as ourselves. Nevertheless, Jelial is traditionally invoked to stir the flames of passion within an established relationship and to ensure fidelity—presumably by keeping the lovers' bed so hot that the partners have no need to look elsewhere.

To pep up the passion in your relationship you can call upon the Angel Jelial to help fan the flames of love. He is drawn by the smell of exotic spices such as cinnamon and ginger, which are also arousing to us. Place a few drops of essential oils in an incense burner and light some candles. Red candles symbolize man and blue candles, woman. They also represent passion and fidelity respectively. Using a pointed instrument, carefully carve Jelial's name in Theban script (see page 116) around the tops of the candles before lighting them. Place passionate red roses in the lovers' chamber too. The best time is a Friday night around 10 o'clock. This is the planetary hour of passionate Mars on the day of loving Venus.

Left: Ginger is an exotic, warming spice that can help us tune into Jelial, Angel of Passion.

The Assisting Angels

Fidelity
Tezalel

O f all the problems that can undermine a love partnership, infidelity is probably the most difficult to overcome. The sense of hurt and betrayal suffered by the injured party can make the restoration of trust very hard to achieve. Sometimes partners drift apart and there is no will to keep the relationship together. This is not necessarily a bad thing, for not all relationships are destined to last. But, if you are determined to hold your relationship together, you can call on certain angels who are specifically there to help.

If you are particularly concerned that you or your partner might stray, then you can call upon the assistance of Tezalel, who is the angel responsible for fidelity in marriage and partnerships. To invoke Tezalel take two blue candles—blue signifies fidelity—and bind them together with copper wire in a figure of eight. Copper is the metal of Venus, and the figure of eight symbolizes eternity. Light the candles and place them in a safe place—they may flare up! Burn some sandalwood and frankincense and recite this prayer, or a similar one, to the four sacred directions, starting in the east.

In the name of the Almighty,
Whose love for us never falters,
I/we invoke you, great Angel Tezalel,
As the Angel of Fidelity,
To bless this relationship.
help us always to stay true to each other
And never stray from each other's side.
May we grow in love together,
Inseparable and strong,
Lovers for all eternity.
I/we thank and honor you
For hearing this my/our prayer,
In the name of the
Almighty.

Attracting a Lover

Theliel

Theliel is an Angel of Love commonly invoked in ritual angel magic to attract a lover, and many magicians have tried to use his assistance to win over the object of their desire.

However, Theliel cannot influence people against their will or interfere in their personal destiny. If you wish to attract a particular person and win their love, Theliel can help bring about the best opportunities to strike the spark of love.

If you simply wish to bring love into your life and have no particular candidate in mind, then Theliel can be relied upon to bring someone most suited to your true needs into your sphere. This person will be suited to you in ways that will not necessarily be immediately apparent.

Theliel is one of the angels of Venus, so the best time to invoke him is on a Friday, preferably during the waxing Moon and ideally at sunrise. Light two pink candles and burn some sandalwood as incense. Recite this, or a similar, prayer of invocation to the four sacred directions, starting in the east and working clockwise.

In the name of the Almighty, Creator of all,
I invoke you, great Angel Theliel,
   Prince of Love,
To help bring a suitable lover into my life;
Someone with whom my love may grow,
That I may grow nearer to that Divine Love,
Which is the source and destiny of my being.
I thank and honor you for hearing this my wish,
In the name of the Almighty.

71

Commitment

habbiel

O ften the most difficult stage in a love relationship is that point where two people have established sufficient intimacy to be "involved," but one or both may be frightened of taking the next step to full commitment. Nowadays there is less social pressure, particularly on women, to get married and have children, and there is no longer a stigma attached to having a series of relationships. Commitment can be more easily delayed.

It is safer for the ego not to commit: it feels less exposed and it can get away with selfish habits that in a shared life could be intolerable. The ego hates the idea of having to change. There may be old wounds or insecurities that stand to be exposed by the greater intimacy that commitment engenders.

An angel who understands all the emotional and psychological intricacies of commitment is Habbiel, an angel of the First Heaven and of Monday, the day of the Moon. The Moon governs the emotions and feelings and also has its dark side, the unconscious. Habbiel can help you or your lover find the trust and courage to open up to the bright, purifying light of committed love. Invoke Habbiel on a Monday, preferably when the Moon is in the sky. Light nine white candles and diffuse the room with a lunar incense such as jasmine. Address your invocation to the four sacred directions, starting in the east and working deosil (clockwise).

In the name of the loving Creator of all,
Who is pure, unconditional light and love,
I call upon you, habbiel, great Angel of Love,
To fill my (and/or your lover's) heart
with the courage and trust
To commit wholeheartedly
To this love we share.
I honor and thank you for hearing my prayer,
In the name of the Almighty.

Chastity
Tahariel

T he love angels have for their Creator and for
humanity is unconditional and unceasing. They
have no need to find a lover for they are lovers
in the highest sense. As St. Thomas Aquinas, the
thirteenth-century philosopher and theologian, said,
"Angels cannot help loving by force of nature." Our idea
of love is often focused on romantic love, which, as we all
know, can be a minefield.

There can come a time in our lives when we want to
retreat from the sometimes hurtful world of romantic
liaison. Celibacy means merely abstaining from sexual
relations. Chastity, however, also suggests purity and a
commitment to the higher, platonic love of the Divine.

The Angel of Purity is Tahariel. He is there to help
us commit to a period—however short—of chastity,
allowing us to purify heart, soul, and body. Before
invoking Tahariel, take a bath, set a white Madonna lily, symbol of pure or
virginal love, on your altar, and light a single white candle. An invocation to
Tahariel should, as always, be addressed to the four sacred directions, starting in
the east. It may go something like this:

*Above: As Angel of
Purity, Tahariel can help
us achieve the highest
ideal of love—a platonic
love of the divine.*

In the name of the Almighty Creator,
From the fire of whose love the angels were born,
I beseech you, Tahariel, Angel of Purity,
    To ignite a purifying fire in my heart
    To purge unworthy thoughts and deeds.
    And allow a purer passion to grow—
    My own true love for One and All.
I thank and honor you for hearing this my
      prayer,
In the name of the Almighty.

Angels of Birth and Death

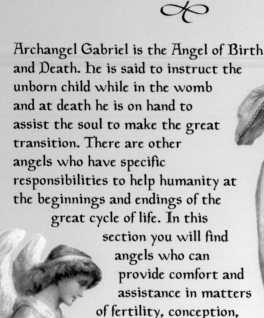

Archangel Gabriel is the Angel of Birth and Death. He is said to instruct the unborn child while in the womb and at death he is on hand to assist the soul to make the great transition. There are other angels who have specific responsibilities to help humanity at the beginnings and endings of the great cycle of life. In this section you will find angels who can provide comfort and assistance in matters of fertility, conception, birth, and death.

Childbirth

Armisael

According to the *Talmud*, a woman in labor should recite *Psalm 20* nine times to ensure an easy birth. As an alternative, you may prefer to call upon angelic assistance. While Gabriel and Temeluch take care of the unborn child in the womb, it is the Angel Armisael who is traditionally called upon to assist with labor. You could plan to handle the situation in advance by writing a letter of petition (see page 120) to Armisael using angelic script before your due date. If further assistance is required or the situation becomes critical, the following invocation can be performed. (If the mother-to-be is unable to perform the invocation herself, it can, of course, be performed on her behalf.)

Green is the color of initiation and childbirth, so first light a green candle. If candle burning is not permitted in the place you are having your baby, visualize a bright green light as you recite these words to the four cardinal points, starting in the east and working deosil (clockwise):

In the name of the Almighty, the Creator of all things,
Creator of us both, I beseech you great Angel
  Armisael,
As protector of mother and child in birth,
To grant this child safe passage
And save (me) the mother from injury
And overwhelming pain.
I honor you and thank you
For performing this your duty,
In the name of the Almighty.

The strength of the invocation can be enhanced by sprinkling saltwater around the labor room beforehand. In case of extreme emergency the Ritual of the Pentagram can be performed (see page 110), calling upon the added assistance of the Four Great Archangels.

Conception
Lailah

T hose who feel ready to take on the great responsibility and sacrifice involved in having children can invoke the help of the Angel Lailah to help them conceive. Lailah is the Angel of Conception, whose energy is very feminine. She is probably synonymous with Lelahiah, in Kabbalistic lore, one of the 72 angels bearing a letter of the Shemhamphora, the mystical name of God. The ideal time to try to conceive when invoking Lailah's help is at night, preferably a Friday night, ideally at New Moon. Obviously, though, the ovarian cycle will be an important guide.

Light three candles, one red and one white, and a green one between them, signifying the child to be born from the union of male and female. Sandalwood is a suitable incense to burn. A prayer of invocation may be recited along these lines:

Above: As Angel of Conception, Lailah can help grant us the gift of a child.

In the name of the Almighty,
Who has given birth to all things,
I invoke you, great Angel Lailah,
As Angel of Conception,
To grant me/us the gift of a child,
Which I/we will love and cherish
And give every opportunity to be its own true self.
I thank and honor you for granting this wish,
In the name of the Almighty.

Fertility
Samandiriel

The blessing of children in a marriage or conjugal partnership is sometimes taken for granted, but for those to whom it seems denied there can be a great sense of sorrow. In earlier times infertility was seen as a curse. The members of the ancient Gnostic sect known as the Mandaeans, which survives to this day in southern Iraq, believes celibacy to be a sin and the procreation of children a religious duty.

The Angel of Fertility, Samandiriel, was therefore regularly invoked. Since Samandiriel is conditioned to Mandaean customs, this ritual includes some of their practices. Eat no meat and avoid addictive substances for at least 24 hours prior to the invocation, which should be performed before sunrise, ideally on the first day of a New Moon. Take a purifying bath and immerse your head three times, face first, as in a ritual baptism. Dress in a simple white silk robe and light three white candles. Sprinkle some saltwater around the edges of the room and burn some frankincense and myrrh. Address your invocation to the north only.

In the name of the Almighty Creator,
Who gives life to all things,
I invoke you Angel, Samandiriel,
With your power to bestow fertility,
To bless us/me with the gift of a child.
This we will raise in the ways of love and truth,
And forever treasure as proof of your great love
For us and for the One who made us all.
I/we honor and thank you for hearing this, our prayer,
In the name of the Almighty.

Bereavement

Yehudiah

The death of a close friend, partner, or relative can be a very painful and difficult experience. First of all we feel a great sense of loss—an important part of our lives has suddenly become part of the past. Did we say and do all the things we could have done? Did that person know how much we loved them? Did we love them enough?

Death can be a great test of faith, particularly when someone dies "before their time," because of accident or disease. We may feel that life seems pointless, arbitrary, or cruel. The bereaved can find themselves denying the reality of a just and loving God, as if death proved life to be meaningless.

It is important to be humble, to remind ourselves that there are great mysteries to life that we cannot expect to understand. When poetry and prayer fail to fill the aching void of grief, we may take comfort in all the ancient traditions that insist on the immortality of the soul. The notion of death as oblivion is a recent product of empty materialism. The transition of the soul can take as long as 49 days, according to Mandaean and Tibetan Buddhist tradition. So the Angel Yehudiah can be invoked, in your own personal way, at any time during this period, to help ensure the safe crossing of your loved one.

Left: The Angel Yehudiah helps guide the souls of the departed to heaven—a great comfort to those who mourn their parting.

Child's Gender

Sandalphon

Sandalphon is widely considered in angel lore to be one of the most important angels in Heaven. He is said to be the twin of Metatron, the ruling angel of Heaven. Legend has it that Sandalphon was once the prophet Elijah, as Metatron was once the prophet Enoch. Sandalphon is personally responsible for the welfare of humankind.

Sandalphon is the angel who decides the gender of a child upon its conception. Should you wish to choose the gender of a hoped-for child, you can enlist his help in the following way. On the night that you hope to conceive, light a candle on your altar. Burn some sandalwood incense and take a bath. Contemplate your reasons for preferring a child of a particular gender and feel the love you would have for this child. Put on a fresh white nightgown and pray to Sandalphon to intercede on your behalf, using the following petition:

Below: The great Sandalphon decides the gender of all children at their conception.

O great and glorious Angel
    Sandalphon,
Who intercedes untiringly on behalf of
    all humanity,
We beseech you in the name of the
    Almighty,
Creator of all above and below,
To grant this, our wish, should we
    conceive this night,
To bless us with a boy/girl child.
Knowing this to be your holy office,
We place our hopes and trust in you,
In the name of the Almighty.

Angels of Grace

Grace, in the religious sense, is a blessing or virtue that elevates us spiritually, rendering us more conscious and closer to God. In this sense such virtues as wisdom, justice, and mercy are graces bestowed upon us by the Almighty through the ministration of his angels. All angels are in a state of grace, existing as they do in loving harmony with the Creator. Some of these angels are able to bestow particular virtues on humanity. It is easier for them to do this if we recognize the value of such virtues, and appeal to their governing angels to help us embody them.

Spiritual Knowledge
haamiah

haamiah is an angel of the Choir of Powers. This choir is responsible for resisting the demons that pervert truth, and is said to protect religions from malign influence. Haamiah is responsible for religious cults and is the protector of those seeking spiritual knowledge.

This is a very important job. Many of us are vulnerable to manipulation by "false prophets" who set themselves up as gurus or spiritual guides. We are also prey to our own weaknesses. We may think we are on a spiritual path when in fact we are merely seeking powers with which to inflate our egos.

Humility is crucial if we are to succeed in our quest for spiritual truth. The Angel Haamiah can guide us on our path and ensure that we are in safe hands. We can invoke him at any time. A single white candle may be lit, and some purifying myrrh can be burned.

Above: When seeking spiritual knowledge we must be sure that our intent is pure.

In the name of the Almighty Creator,
 Whose truth is universal and absolute,
 I call upon you, great Angel haamiah,
 With an honest and open heart,
 To guide me in my quest for spiritual knowledge.
May I know the true from the false,
And may I not be misled by deceivers.
 I honor you and thank you for granting me your protection,
 As is your righteous duty.
 In the name of the Almighty.

Wisdom

Sagnessagiel

Above: Sagnessagiel is said by the prophet Enoch to be the mighty Angel Metatron in his aspect as the Prince of Wisdom.

Sagnessagiel is the Prince of Wisdom. Enoch lists his name as one of the many names of Metatron, considered in some traditions as the highest-ranking angel, Prince of the Seraphim, and Guardian of Humanity.

Wisdom differs from knowledge in important respects. To be knowledgeable is to have accumulated many facts and details through learning. To be wise, on the other hand, is to have the gift of understanding, good judgment based on intelligence and experience.

If we wish for greater wisdom in order to perceive the mysteries of life, or better judgment in our day-to-day lives, then we can invoke the great Angel Sagnessagiel to bestow some of this grace upon us.

> In the name of the Almighty Creator,
> Whose wisdom is faultless and absolute,
> I invoke you, great Angel Sagnessagiel,
> And humbly implore you to give me the grace
> Of greater understanding.
> May I lead my life more wisely
> And see things as they really are,
> I honor and thank you for hearing this, my prayer,
> In the name of the Almighty.

This invocation, or one of your own should be addressed to the four sacred directions working east, south, west, and north. Burn some sage and light nine candles—nine being symbolic of truth, which is the reward of the wise.

Patience

Achaiah

Achaiah is is the Angel of Patience. Impatience is such a common affliction that we take it for granted. Whenever things don't move along as quickly or as smoothly as we would wish we are liable to frown or grimace in frustration. Impatience stems from our desire to control things, a reluctance to go with the flow. We should really welcome the chance to slow down and take more notice of the world around us.

Achaiah is also called the Discoverer of the Secrets of Nature—another clue to the merits of patience. Patience allows us the time to observe and recognize the natural rhythms and patterns of things. And appreciation is a magical two-way process, for nature loves to take us into her confidence if she feels esteemed.

If you would like to let go of all the frustration and tension that goes with impatience, call upon the Angel Achaiah to help you. You don't have to write him a petition or perform an invocation, just learn to observe yourself and, whenever you catch yourself getting impatient, slow down, close your eyes for a second, and breathe the name Achaiah. Imagine him winking at you with a wise, knowing smile, then open your eyes, take a breath, and slip into the flow. You'll soon get the hang of it.

Peace
Seraphiel

V arious angels have been accorded the title Prince of Peace, but the greatest of these is Seraphiel, chief of the highest-ranking angelic choir, the Seraphim. The Seraphim are the angels of love and light who guard the throne of God. They are therefore the closest to the ineffable "Peace of God that Passeth Understanding."

Few mortals have ever beheld the dazzling presence of a Seraph, and their presence cannot be evoked. The following ritual, however, can help one reach a seraphic state of divine contemplation. Choose a moment when you are feeling peaceful. Take a relaxing bath and make yourself comfortable. Burn your favorite incense and light a single white candle. Place it in front of you with the flame at eye level. Say a simple prayer in gratitude for all your blessings and in recognition of the infinite love of God. Then, close your eyes and allow the afterimage of the flame to fill your whole being with peaceful, loving light. Let the light become ever brighter, without becoming uncomfortable. Imagine the light to be made up of a myriad of angels of peace uplifting you into the Divine Presence. This ritual is best performed at night, allowing you to drift off to sleep after what can be an extraordinarily uplifting experience.

Left: The prophet Enoch describes Seraphiel as the most dazzling of the heavenly angels.

Freedom
Terathel

T erathel is an Angel of Light of the Choir of Dominions. His special concern is the freedom of individuals and the advancement of civilization among the nations of Earth. There are still so many places in the world where people have no real freedom, and even in the developed nations we see countless examples of social injustice.

We can do more to help, however, by transmuting our anger into compassion. Even when things seem to be patently unfair, it is important to resist the urge to rail against the heavens. Hard though it is to accept, the fact is that everything is right. Everything unfolds just the way it has to and is part of a pattern far more meaningful than we can imagine. But we can actively serve the goal of progress by invoking the Angel Terathel to help guide societies and their leaders along the path of freedom.

Above: Terathel is an angel of the Choir of Dominions. he propagates light, civilization, and liberty.

In the name of our Almighty Creator,
Through whom all things have their being,
I invoke you, great Angel Terathel,
Chosen as you are to assist humanity
On the path of individual and communal freedom,
To guide the hearts and minds of those who lead us
In all the nations and places of the Earth,
That they may be inspired to work for the common good.
I thank and honor you for the service you perform,
In the name of the Almighty.

Justice

Vasiariah

V asiariah is a member of the Choir of
Dominions under Zadkiel. He is an
Angel of Justice and the patron angel
of the legal profession. Vasiariah can be
petitioned or invoked to assist those who are to
be judged before the law. He cannot interfere
with the legal system and cannot make someone
innocent when they are guilty.

What he can do is ensure that the correct verdict is reached and, in the case of
guilt, he can encourage the court to be merciful and show clemency. Sometimes it
is not in the best interests of a person to escape the punishment they have deserved
through their actions. They may allow themselves to feel that they "got away with
it" and have even less respect for the law. Vasiariah understands the subtleties of
crime and punishment and, if called upon to influence a legal proceeding, will not
encourage an especially lenient sentence to be passed unless he feels that the
accused has learned his or her lesson.

Divine Law is concerned less with punishment than contrition, which is the
remorse that comes from recognizing our wrongdoing and the resolve to change
our ways. If we wish to appeal to Vasiariah for mercy, either for ourselves or someone
else, we can write him a petition as
outlined on page 120.

Right: As an Angel of Justice,
Vasiariah can help ensure that courts
of law reach correct verdicts and
apply leniency where appropriate.

Compassion
Rahmiel

C ompassion is one of the greatest of all the virtues associated with angels. Compassion is what moves us with pity for the sufferings of another. It is easy to feel compassion for a starving child or an injured puppy, but it requires angelic understanding to realize that the most horrible people are the ones most lacking in love.

The Angel Rahmiel is one of two angels of compassion, along with the Archangel Raphael, and he is closely associated with that most compassionate and humble of saints, St. Francis of Assisi. St. Francis was an aristocratic young medieval playboy, who one day encountered a leper while riding in the countryside. He was stricken with such overwhelming compassion that he thenceforth gave up everything to heal the sick and minister to the needy. He empathized so completely with the suffering of Jesus that he famously received the stigmata—bleeding at the points where Christ's body was pierced. Upon his death he is said to have become an angel himself and to have been renamed Rahmiel.

As a member of the Choir of Virtues, Rahmiel may have been one of the two Angels of Ascension

Above: St. Francis of Assisi receives the stigmata, a symbol of his compassion for the sufferings of Jesus on the cross.

that escorted Christ to Heaven. If we wish to stop harming ourselves and our fellow mortals by judging and condemning those poor souls that are lost in vice, we can pray to the Angel Rahmiel to fill us with the sweetness of his infinite compassion, that we may empathize with the plight of all beings that are separated from love.

Angels of Mercy

The great Angel of Mercy is Archangel Gabriel, who can always be called upon to intercede on behalf of us or others when we are in need. There are other angels, however, who have specific dominion over certain phenomena, such as natural disasters. These angels can be invoked to mitigate the destruction such disasters can cause, and to protect those threatened by them. Yet other angels can provide the relief these disasters necessitate. Some people, who have certain abilities and qualities, are said to be able to aid the assisting angels while in their astral bodies. May more of us aspire to such magical charity.

Hurricanes

Zamiel

h urricanes wreak terrible havoc, resulting in great damage to homes and property and, far worse, to loss of human life. Such "acts of God" are impossible to stop, but their effects can certainly be mitigated through prayer and, in individual cases, miracles can occur that save the lives of people caught and apparently doomed by these terrible storms.

The Angel Zamiel has dominion over hurricanes and can be invoked to protect certain endangered individuals or to mitigate the effect of such storms. When you hear of a potentially deadly hurricane you can invoke the mercy of Zamiel with a prayer of invocation such as the following:

> In the name of the all-powerful Creator,
> I invoke you, great Angel Zamiel,
> As the Angel of hurricanes,
> To calm the fury of this terrible storm;
> May you divert its path from the most vulnerable places
> To blow itself out where few can come to harm.
> I honor and thank you for hearing my prayer,
> In the name of the Almighty.

Your invocation should be addressed to the four winds, starting in the east and working deosil (clockwise). Any number of candles may be burned. Visualize the calm eye of the storm and imagine it drawing in the winds spiraling around it, calming them until all is still and peaceful.

Right: The spiral vortex of a
hurricane, one of the most
devastating forces of nature.

Protection against *Evil*

Lahabiel

I n all traditional cultures there is a prevalent belief in evil spirits. Misfortunes, madness, and sicknesses are attributed to their malign attentions, and all manner of charms and amulets may be employed to ward them off. Sorcerers and malefactors are believed to employ such spirits, but even without them the power of their projected thoughts can be strong enough to cause harm.

In the developed countries we live in less superstitious times and find it more comforting to believe that rational explanations can be found for unpleasant situations. No one can tell us with certainty what the truth really is in such matters. As individuals we may have our own views, based on experience, belief, or intuition. If you feel in some way "spooked," or that something's "eating you," it may be worth looking for some psychic or spiritual protection.

One of the angels most commonly invoked to ward off evil spirits is Lahabiel, an angel of the First Day, Sunday, who works under Archangel Michael the Dragonslayer. Lahabiel has specific duties as a "jinxbuster," and he can be a powerful ally. The best time to petition or invoke him is on a Sunday. The best ritual to invoke the protection of Lahabiel is the Ritual of the Pentagram, which is described on page 110. Alternatively, you could write Lahabiel's name in Theban script (see page 116) on a piece of leather and wear it on your person as a protective amulet.

Left: The forces of good
banish the forces of evil
personified by Satan in this
Gustave Doré engraving.

Drought

Riddia

Above: Rain is the giver of fertility and life. It also restores life.

R ain is the water of life, without which no living plant or creature on Earth could survive. Not surprisingly, therefore, all cultures and traditions have had deities or spirits that ruled the rain, which they would invoke with—often complex—rituals to guard against drought.

There are various angels that traditionally rule the rain. Probably the best known among them is Riddia, greatly revered in Hebrew lore as the Prince of Rain and Ruler of Water. In times of drought, Riddia can be invoked to bring rain. If this is to apply to a place other than where you live, you can adapt the following invocation naming the place in question. You can also draw a rough map of the place, write its name in the middle, and sprinkle drops of water on it for rain or salt for dryness. Light nine white or silver candles and burn camphor or jasmine for rain.

In the name of the Almighty Creator,
Provider of all that sustains life,
I invoke you, Riddia, Prince of Rain,
To bring refreshment to this parched earth,
That the plants and crops might grow
And feed all creatures that live here.
I honor and thank you with open heart
For hearing this, my prayer,
In the name of the Almighty.

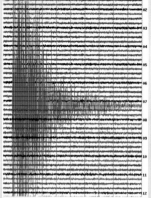

Earthquakes

Suiel

The Earth is still evolving, still giving birth, shifting and contracting. This poses dangers for those who live on its surface. Earthquakes occur with a terrifying suddenness and the survival of those caught in the epicenter is in the lap of the angels. Seismologists, scientists who study earthquakes, are working hard to develop early-warning systems to try to anticipate the occurrence of such seismic disruptions.

It seems that our relatives in the animal kingdom are much more sensitive than our best instruments to the onset of earthquakes, sometimes many hours or even days ahead. We must hope that they may be able to help us. In the meantime, those who live along established fault lines remain at risk.

The fact is that all of us owe our every waking moment to the grace of God. Part of the way of truth and humility lies in accepting this without fear or complaint. Nevertheless, we can help protect ourselves and others by communicating with the angels. An angel who traditionally has dominion over earthquakes is Suiel. We can invoke him to ward off or mitigate the effects of such catastrophes. To invoke Suiel we can light four white candles, symbolizing hope and stability. We can also burn a little myrrh.

In the name of the Almighty Creator,
Who allows all things to be,
I invoke you, great Angel Suiel,
As Ruler of Earthquakes,
To provide the means of warning,
Against impending upheaval.
May you ease the birth pangs of Mother Earth,
That she shudder less violently.
May you guide our builders to build more safely.
I honor you and thank you for your mercy.

Famine

Asda

Famine, that most biblical of afflictions, is still a reality in many of the poorer parts of the world, particularly in places that regularly suffer from drought or flooding. It is sobering to consider that the developed nations may be contributing to such disasters through their profligate burning of fossil fuels, creating the "greenhouse effect" that alters climate patterns. We can help make up for this by contributing aid and supplies. We can also petition the angels to do the same.

The Angel of Nourishment is Asda, sometimes called Isda. This Angel of Mercy can help provide us with our daily bread. We can call upon him to tend to those who are starving, ensuring that as many of them as possible receive enough nourishment to stay alive. Asda can make a little food go a long way. He may even have assisted Jesus in the Feeding of the Five Thousand. Certainly, this is the kind of miracle he can perform. To help make an invocation to Asda effective we can place a handful of cereal grains on our altar and light four green candles, symbolic of the Earth and growth. We can also burn some sandalwood incense.

> In the name of the Almighty Creator,
> On whom we depend for our daily bread,
> I beseech you, Asda, great Angel of Nourishment,
> To put sustenance in the mouths of the starving,
> Wherever they may be on Earth.
> May they survive and prosper and know that
> The greatest food for heart and soul is love.
> I honor you and thank you for hearing this prayer,
> In the name of the Almighty.

93

Angels of healing

❧

The great Archangel Raphael, the "Shining One Who heals," rules over all matters governing health. He can be called upon to help overcome any health problem, but he also has various helper angels, who work through him and specialize in specific problems. You will find some of the better-known ones in the pages that follow. The more astrologically minded may wish to work with the Planetary Angels (see pages 40–57), whose planets rule different body parts and functions, or you can work with both—you can never have too many angels on your side!

Heart

Och

O ch is a favorite angel in occult angelology. As the Angel of Alchemy, he can provide the knowledge and understanding required by those undertaking the Great Work. As the guardian of the Elixir of Life, he can extend the lives of those who successfully invoke him. He is a Prince of the Sun, under Archangel Michael, and is said to rule 36,536 legions of solar spirits.

The Sun rules the heart, and Och is the angel to call upon to keep it healthy. The heart is not only the vital organ that circulates the blood around the body, but is also the seat of the soul. Spiritual growth is dependent on how much we care, our will to love—how much heart we have. Och understands all the mysteries of the heart and can assist in all cardiac problems, as well as less obviously organic matters of the heart.

Och should be invoked on a Sunday, preferably at noon, when the Sun is at its zenith. Light six white, yellow, or gold candles and burn some frankincense, myrrh, or copal. The following prayer, or something similar, should be addressed to all four corners, starting in the east and working deosil (clockwise).

Great Angel Och, to whom it is given,
By the grace of the One, Creator of all,
To know the mysterious ways of the heart,
I beseech you to fill this heart up with healing,
I implore you to fill this heart up with love,
That it may beat strongly for as long
as it can do,
In time with the Truth of Below
and Above.
In the name of the all-loving Almighty.

Left: There are many angels of healing, some of whom specialize in particular problems. All can be petitioned to bring relief to the suffering.

95

Eyesight
Mahzian

Little has been written about the Angel Mahzian, but tradition has long recognized him as the angel to invoke in order to restore or improve eyesight. To achieve the best results it is worth considering some astro-alchemical

Above: The Angel Mahzian can be petitioned to restore our eyesight and so our ability to observe and contemplate Creation's plenitude.

lore in connection with the eyes. The Sun rules the right eye of man and the left eye of woman, while the Moon rules the left eye of man and the right eye of woman. So, whether the left, right, or both eyes need healing, the best time to invoke the help of Mahzian is at sunrise on the day of the Full Moon.

There is a good chance that the Moon will still be above the horizon as the Sun's first rays appear, allowing one the greatest benefits of both these heavenly bodies. Rise before dawn and take a purifying bath or shower. Just as the Sun's first rays are about to appear over the eastern horizon, face the east and recite these words. (You may, of course, use your own words if you wish.)

> In the name of the Almighty, Creator of all that is,
> I beseech you great Angel Mahzian,
> As restorer of the gift of sight,
> To grant me the vision that I lack.
> I honor and thank you with all my heart
> For performing this, your duty,
> In the name of the Almighty, our Creator.

Now turn to the south and repeat the prayer, then do the same to the west and the north. If you have one, or can borrow one, an eagle's feather, symbolizing sharpness of vision, can be used during the ritual. Gently brush your weak eye or eyes with it as you recite the prayer.

General Healing
Ariel

Ariel's name means "Lion of God," and he is often visualized with a lion's head. Although some authorities have called him a fallen angel, he is generally accepted in Jewish tradition to be one of Raphael's most important helpers in the task of healing sickness in the human realm. The lion is a symbol of the Sun—hence the Zodiac sign of Leo, which is ruled by the Sun. The Sun represents vitality and wellness of being. Ariel is therefore the healing angel to call upon if you are suffering from low energy or general debilitation. In such cases it is worth invoking the help of Ariel with a prayer along the following lines:

In the name of the Almighty Creator of all,
I call upon you, Ariel, great Angel of healing,
Ordained to restore health to mortals,
To give me vitality and well-being,
That I may be fitter to walk my path
In the way of truth and love.
I honor and thank you for hearing this, my prayer,
In the name of the Almighty.

To enhance this invocation you can burn some copal ("lion's tears") and burn six candles: white, yellow, or beeswax.

Left: A healing angel brings a healing draft to a sick and weary woman.

97

Curing Disease

Sabrael

I n most traditional cultures, diseases are believed to be caused by evil spirits lodged in the body. There is increasing scientific evidence to suggest that the majority of diseases are caused by viruses or parasites entering the body. The analogy is obvious, if alarming. It is quite possible that the fallen angels govern unpleasant parasitical organisms that literally suck the life out of their hosts. In occult angelology there is said to be only one angel that can defeat Sphendonael, the demon of disease. That angel is Sabrael, one of the "Shining Ones," or Choir of Virtues. In cases of disease, Sabrael can be invoked to root out any demonic impulse or infestation.

Cloves

As Sabrael must engage in combat, the best day to invoke him is a Tuesday, when he can use the martial energies harnessed by Camael as the ruler of Mars (see page 50). Strong purging and purifying scents should be burned, such as wormwood and cloves. Light five red candles and face the east to recite this invocation.

In the name of the Almighty, Creator of all,
I invoke you, great shining Angel Sabrael,
To drive the demon of disease from me/................(fill in name)
May your fiery sword bring purifying light to every cell in
   my/................ body,
So that there may be no place for disease to hide.
May my/................ resistance be strengthened to repel all
   invasion and keep my/his/her body a temple of love.
I honor and thank you for doing your duty,
In the name of the Almighty.

Memory

Zachariel

Zachariel is a regent prince of the Second Heaven and the Choir of Dominions. He has traditionally been invoked to grant the gift of a good memory. While Gabriel, as planetary ruler of the Moon, governs the mechanics of the brain, which include the faculty of memory, and Cassiel rules long-term memory, Zachariel can improve the quality of memory. Memory is a crucial function, not just as an organizing tool to remind us what and where things are, but as fair witness of all we have experienced. The heart works directly with the memory, recalling how we have been and what we have done, in order that we can recognize our faults and change for the better.

Achieving greater consciousness is the goal of all seekers. Then our awareness can be fully informed by our store of knowledge, knowledge that the heart can then transmute into wisdom. This is the quality of memory that Zachariel can afford us.

> In the name of the Almighty Creator,
> Who gives consciousness to all living things,
> I beseech you, great Angel Zachariel,
> Who is given by the One to govern the quality of memory,
> To impart to me depth and clarity of recall,
> That I may be fair witness to all I experience,
> For the good of all and the harm of none.
> I honor and thank you for granting me this wish,
> In the name of the Almighty.

This invocation is enhanced by burning white candles and burning rosemary—herb or oil—as this plant can restore memory and is sacred to Zachariel.

Rosemary

Angels of the World

❧

Angels are the governing intelligences behind
everything in Creation, from the stars and galaxies
down to the most mundane of human activities. The
angels in this section govern everyday matters, which
are no less important in the great scheme of things
than the great trials of birth and death. There are
great truths to be found even in apparent trivialities.
The desire to do something well, whatever it is, is
what gives us our grace. If we can love where we are,
love whom we're with, and love what we are doing,
then we are blessed, and so is everything around us.

Business Ventures

Teoael

When we're starting a new business venture, an element of luck, as well as hard work and a good business plan, is needed. Unseen factors can undermine even the most surefire business idea. People starting new businesses often invest a lot of money—their own or other people's—as well as their own hopes, time, and energy. The stakes can be high and the rewards of failure bitter, leaving relationships, as well as finances, in tatters.

In traditional Jewish communities the Angel Teoael was often invoked to protect ships carrying valuable cargoes. In the days of sail, a merchant could be ruined if his goods ended up at the bottom of the sea or in the hands of pirates. Teoael is a prince of the Choir of Thrones and is petitioned to bless new business ventures to help ensure their success. To write a petition to Teoael, follow the instructions given on page 120. Write the petition on your company's letterhead and/or include in the envelope a business card and anything else that may help him tune in. Bear in mind

Above: The Angel Teoael is traditionally invoked or petitioned to bring success to new business ventures.

that the nature of your business and the intent behind it will not be irrelevant to Teoael. As an angel of light and love he can support only positive initiatives.

107

Exams

Raphael

Written or oral examinations can often be the source of great anxiety and tension. Many weeks, months, or even years of study can be judged by one's ability to perform well in a crucial couple of hours or less on a particular day. This requires confidence, calmness, and good powers of recall.

Nervous tension can undermine everything. Some people break out in sweats, their minds seize up, and they find it hard to even speak or hold a pen. These are extreme cases, but, when your whole future seems to be on the line, it is worth ensuring that you've got everything going for you.

The great Archangel Raphael, in his role as planetary ruler of Mercury, is probably the best angel to invoke or petition prior to taking exams. Raphael rules the mental processes—the ability to think straight and communicate well, and the powers of recall necessary to access information that has been stored in the mind.

Raphael has quicksilver mental reflexes, and this is what we need to do ourselves justice in exam conditions.

To petition Raphael, follow the instructions on page 120. Invocations and petitions should be on a Wednesday. Raphael responds very quickly, so petitions should be burned after a week. If you wish to make an invocation to Raphael, follow the guidelines set out on page 41.

Finding Lost Objects

Rochel

Most traditional cultures have a deity or spirit that is invoked to help find things. In the Catholic Church, St. Anthony is the patron saint of lost objects and is regularly called upon for this purpose, particularly in Latin America. The angel who bears this particular responsibility is Rochel.

Before you petition Rochel to help you find something that has been lost or mislaid, it is important to consider first your attachment to the item in question. What is its value to you? Why is it important that it be found? Sometimes when we lose things, we can become suspicious that someone may have stolen them. We may start to suspect our friends and family. Don't do it. If they say they haven't got it, accept it. Suspicion is a demon we should not entertain. Far better to let something go, forget about it, than to project such a divisive emotion onto the people around us.

We can write a petition to Rochel stating why our lost item is valuable to us or why it is important that we find it. The petition will be particularly effective if you write it in Theban script, as outlined on page 116. Make a little drawing of the item in question or pop a corresponding object in the envelope with it—such as the partner of a lost earring. The trick now is to forget about it, let it go. If you can do this, you will be amazed how often something will reappear as if by magic.

Sports
Camael

All sports and competitive games are ruled by Camael, Regent of Mars, the planet of competition. Camael understands that competition inspires excellence. Without it we would lack the passion to strive to be the best. Competition raises the standard of skill required to be a winner. It makes us run faster, throw further, play better. Mars rules the blood, which feeds oxygen to the muscles, giving an athlete strength, flexibility, and stamina.

Camael channels the aggression of Mars into healthy physical expression. In team sports and contact sports, competitiveness and aggression are virtues if well channeled. Camael can help summon the courage and self-belief necessary for athletes to excel. An attribute that often marks a champion is the ability to stay focused in the heat of the moment, to resist the pressure and tension, and produce the big jump, or make the great shot just when it counts.

Mars is the planet of iron, and Camael can help us develop the iron will necessary to bring the very best out of ourselves in all situations, and triumph where others crumble. Simply meditating on the attributes of Camael can improve your performance, but, for the big occasions, or to achieve a breakthrough, it is worth invoking him to assist directly. Refer to page 51 for Camael's correspondences and to page 41 for a suggested invocation ritual.

Left: Camael can help channel aggression into a healthy competitiveness that inspires sporting excellence.

Gardening
habuhiah

habuhiah is the Angel of Gardening, Agriculture, and Soil Fertility. Every type of plant has a *deva*, an angelic intelligence that is responsible for its form and characteristics. Habuhiah works closely with these *devas*, encouraging them to make their plants succulent and nutritious for us to eat. It makes sense for the plants, too, for the ones that grow best and that we find the most nutritious are the ones we prize the most and plant most widely, thus ensuring the survival of the species.

Plants are like children. Children love candy, soda, and fast food even though they are not good for them. They may give them a quick energy boost, but can make them hyperactive and weaken their immune system. Just so with plants. If we feed them chemical fertilizer they may appear to grow faster and more luxuriantly, but they are less robust and nutritious. This upsets the *devas*, who see the inherent

qualities of their charges being undermined. Habuhiah can help us keep the *devas* happy—and ourselves well fed—by working with us to feed the plants and soil well. If you grow your own vegetables, you should try to establish a compost heap made of all your household's organic waste. Every time you add some more scraps to the heap you can invoke Habuhiah to help transform refuse into that miraculous, life-giving substance, compost. And the *devas* will love you.

Left: Farmers and gardeners can work with habuhiah to improve the fertility of their soil and the health of their plants and crops.

RITUALS

⁓

THE VALUE OF RITUAL LIES IN ITS ABILITY TO FOCUS OUR WHOLE BEING AND TUNE IN TO THE OBJECT OF OUR INTENT. THIS IS ACHIEVED THROUGH REPETITION (CENTURIES OF THE SAME RITUAL BEING PERFORMED FOR THE SAME REASON GIVE THE PROCEDURE POWERFUL ENERGETIC CHARACTERISTICS) AND THROUGH ASSOCIATION (USING CORRESPONDING SOUNDS, COLORS, SUBSTANCES, AND OBJECTS TO TUNE INTO A SPECIFIC ENERGETIC ARCHETYPE OR ENTITY). HERE WE WILL FOCUS ON THE MOST STRAIGHTFORWARD TECHNIQUES OF ANGEL MAGIC AND INCLUDE SOME IMPORTANT AND POWERFUL RITUALS, THREE OF WHICH ARE SEALED TO PROTECT THEM FROM THE PROFANE.

Invocation Rituals

❧

Invocation rituals are more effective if we are properly prepared. It is easier to tune in to angelic consciousness if we have purified ourselves and are in touch with our higher Self, the wise, unselfish part of our consciousness. Purification consists of mental preparation, fasting, and cleansing. Fasting can mean abstaining from solid food (but not liquids!) for a day or two (longer is not advised, unless you are used to it) or simply eating less and avoiding animal protein for at least 24 hours. Addictive and stimulating substances should be avoided as far as possible, again for at least 24 hours.

The purpose of fasting is to relax the whole system and calm our energy. For this reason all sexual activity should also be avoided during the purification period. We should try to keep our minds relaxed, avoiding selfish thoughts and quietly counting our blessings. We can drink soothing herb teas such as chamomile, vervain, and mint. Vervain is also a very good addition to a purifying bath—in the form of tea or essential oil. It relaxes and tones the nervous system, and is used to promote clairvoyant dreams. This makes it ideal for work with angels. Baths are also ideal for working with the Planetary Angels. They can be colored and scented correspondingly. In fact a scented, candlelit bath can be recommended as highly conducive to connecting with angelic energies. It may become your preferred setting for conducting invocations.

Left: Soothing herb teas can help us relax, promoting inner peace and deeper meditation when fasting.

Ritual *of the* Pentagram

T he five-pointed star of the pentagram is an ancient symbol of protection and good luck. It represents the five senses, man as microcosm—the image of God. In Christianity, it represents the five redeeming wounds of Christ. It was engraved on a ring delivered from Heaven to King Solomon by the Archangel Raphael to help him build The Temple.

It is the basis of the most widely practiced ritual in the Western Mysteries, used to focus and contain spiritual energy prior to the performance of an invocation. It invokes the Four Great Archangels with four of the holy names of God, to form a circle of power, much like the Medicine Wheel in Native American tradition.

The Ritual

Sprinkle your ritual space with saltwater and burn some of the angels' favorite incense—copal or frankincense and myrrh. First we draw the Kabbalistic Cross of Light. Stand facing the east and imagine a brilliant and infinite white light above you. Raise your right hand above your head and draw the light down to your forehead as you say:

Left: To begin invoking the
Four Great Archangels, stand
facing east.

Thine, O Lord ...

Draw the light down in a line
through your body as you point
toward your feet, saying:

Is the kingdom ...

The line of light follows your hand
as you bring it up to your right
shoulder, saying:

The power ...

Draw the line straight across to your left shoulder, saying:

And the glory ...

Now cup your hands to your heart, seeing and feeling the great
cross of light running through you, and say:

For ever. Amen

Now, still facing the east, point with your right hand (this time you
can use your left hand if you wish), arm outstretched, to a point
slightly higher than your head. Now trace a pentagram, in a
continuous line, starting at the bottom left corner (see diagram
above) and imagining it as a line of fire. Now point at the center
of the blazing pentagram, saying:

> **In the name of the Almighty Yod-heh-Vow-heh
> And Archangel Raphael, Prince of Air,
> I draw this circle in the east.**

Keeping your arm raised, turn to the south, tracing 90 degrees of a
circle of flame. Now trace another pentagram in the same way.

Again, point to the center of the pentagram, saying:

In the name of the Almighty Ah–Don–Ai And Archangel Michael, Prince of Light, I draw this circle in the south.

Keeping your arm raised, turn to the west, tracing another 90 degrees of a circle of flame. Now trace another pentagram in the same way. Again, point to the center of the pentagram, saying:

Above: By preparing adequately for a ritual, we focus our mental and spiritual energy and ensure our invocation will be as effective as possible.

In the name of the Almighty Eh-Ee-Yay
And Archangel Gabriel, Prince of Water,
I draw this circle in the west.

Keeping your arm raised, turn to the north, tracing another 90 degrees of a circle of flame. Now trace another pentagram in the same way. Again, point to the center of the pentagram, saying:

In the name of the Almighty Ag-Yu-La
And Archangel Uriel, Prince of Earth,
I draw this circle in the north.

Keeping your arm raised, turn once more to the east, completing the circle of flame, which now surrounds you with the flaming stars at each cardinal point. Now open wide your arms and say:

Before me Raphael
(visualized as a great yellow light with a violet aura)
Behind me Gabriel
(visualized as a great blue light with an orange aura)
On my right Michael
(visualized as a great red light with a green aura)
On my left Uriel
(visualized as a great green light with a reddish brown aura)
Above me the Father
(visualize a six-pointed star of two interlocking triangles)
Below me the Mother (another six-pointed star)
Within me the Eternal Flame

You are now within a protected sacred space and may perform an invocation to the angel of your choice. Movement within the circle should always be deosil (clockwise). At the end of the ritual perform the Kabbalistic Cross again, as at the beginning.

Dawn Ritual

T his powerful invocation can reveal to the petitioner deep insights into divine mysteries and grant the fulfillment of prayers. It is conducted at dawn, just before sunrise. The great Seraph Vehuhiah, who rules the first rays of the rising Sun, is called upon to answer one's prayers. Then Urzla, a glorious angel of the east and revealer of sacred mysteries, is invoked.

This ritual can be performed on any day of the year, but is particularly powerful on the days that mark the cycles of the solar year—the equinoxes and solstices. The old solar festival of Beltane (May 1) would be another good choice. The most important factor, though, is that it should be a clear dawn so that you can see the sunrise. The ritual should be performed alone, the petitioner having undergone a purifying period of at least 24 hours, as outlined on page 108. It is best conducted in the open air, ideally in a peaceful spot with a clear eastern horizon.

Rise well before dawn to give you time to wash and dress—ideally in natural white cloth—and get to your chosen spot a few minutes before sunrise. Begin by performing a Kabbalistic Cross, as described at the start of the Pentagram Ritual on page 110. Then address the Archangels of the four cardinal points, starting in the east. Raise both arms toward the east and say:

> Great Archangel Raphael,
> Prince of Air and Lord of the East, hail!

Keeping your arms raised, turn to the south and say:

> Great Archangel Michael,
> Prince of Fire and Lord of the South, hail!

Keeping your arms raised, turn to the west and say:

> Great Archangel Gabriel,
> Prince of Water and Lord of the West, hail!

Keeping your arms raised, turn to the north and say:

> Great Archangel Uriel,
> Prince of Earth and Lord of the North, hail!

With arms still raised return to the east, completing the circle. Bow your head to the brightening horizon and let your arms come down to your sides. As soon as the first rays of the Sun appear over the horizon, raise your arms again, saying:

> Hail Vehuhiah, oh Great Shining Seraph!
> hear this, my prayer, in the name of Our Lord.
> I pray that.............................
> I honor and thank you, O Seraph, in the hope
> That you will answer this, my prayer,
> In the name of the Most high.

Lower your arms and bow toward the sun. Relax and let the intent of your words ripple upon the air and be carried by the Sun's brightening rays. Now raise your arms to the east again and say:

> Hail Urzla, glorious Angel of the East!
> hear this, my prayer, in the name of the Lord.
> Please reveal unto me a bright jewel of wisdom
> From the crown of the One who is All Understanding,
> To help me surrender to the light of his love.
> I honor and thank you for this gracious gift,
> In the name of the Most high.

Lower your arms and bow your head, cupping your hands to your heart as if to hold the angel's gift. Stay with the silence for a moment and let the light flood your whole being. The nature of Urzla's gift may not be revealed to you immediately, but if you plant it with care in your heart it will germinate and blossom into an eternal rose of wisdom. Conclude the ritual by addressing the Archangels of the four cardinal points again, exactly as before, but adding "and farewell!" to the "Hail!" This is a powerful ritual, which should be performed only once you are familiar with performing invocations.

Angelic Script

Tradition tells that the angels have their own language, which is similar, but not identical, to Hebrew. There are various versions of the alphabet used for this language, the most straightforward of which is the Theban Script. This is the easiest for us to use, because it is the most similar to our own. Although the characters are quite different, we can simply substitute them for our own letters. You will notice that three letters are lacking—J, U, and W. For J, we use the Theban character for I; for U, the Theban V; and for W, we write the Theban V twice. Words should be transcribed phonetically, for example "enough" would be spelled "enuf".

Below left: Three examples of angelic writing, each corresponding to the 22 letters of the hebrew alphabet.

The Theban Alphabet

A   B   C   D   E

F   G   H   I   K

L   M   N   O   P

Q   R   S   T   V

X   Y   Z

Invoking *Ritual* of the *Pentagram*

This ritual is another version of the pentagram ritual described on pages 110-113. It differs in one very important respect. It begins an invocation by tracing the pentagram in the opposite direction to the protective, "banishing pentagram." This is known as the "invoking pentagram," and makes the circle a powerful attracting force. This can draw in energies and spirits that the inexperienced practitioner may find alarming, even though they cannot harm you directly—unless you ask them to!

Using the invoking pentagram places more responsibility on the shoulders of the petitioner, who then has to "release" any spirits unwittingly, or carelessly, bound by the invocation ceremony. For these reasons, the invoking pentagram should not be used until you have the necessary confidence that only experience can provide.

The invoking ceremony should be performed exactly as outlined on pages 110-113, beginning with the Kabbalistic Cross. The only difference, initially, is that the pentagrams should be traced differently. The invoking pentagram is drawn from the apex down to the left "foot," then across to the right "arm" and so on. Otherwise the procedure is the same.

Following your invocation to the angel of your choice you should perform the banishing ritual of the pentagram, exactly as described on

Left: The Pentagram, or five-pointed star, is a symbol of knowledge and a means of obtaining power and casting spells.

pages 110-113. The only difference is the wording of the last line addressed to each direction. For example, in the east, where you start, you say:

> In the name of the Almighty
> Yod-heh-Vow-heh
> And Archangel Raphael, Prince of Air,
> I banish this circle in the east.

Turning to the south you do the same, concluding: "I banish this circle in the south." And likewise to the west and north. When you arrive back facing east again say:

> In the name of the Almighty Creator,
> I thank you, Great Archangels
> Raphael, Michael, Gabriel, and Uriel,
> For gracing this ritual with your holy presence.
> Hail and Farewell!

Finally you turn a full circle widdershins (counterclockwise) to dissolve the circle, and the ceremony is concluded.

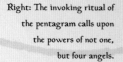

Right: The invoking ritual of
the pentagram calls upon
the powers of not one,
but four angels.

Writing a Petition

A petition is a request or wish written in the form of a prayer. Petitions written in angelic script have more resonance and are more clearly understood by the angel we choose to address. The act of writing a petition involves more concentrated effort and petitions therefore carry more of our energy.

To write a petition to an angel, we should first establish which angel is responsible for the matter in hand. For example, if we wish to attract a lover we should petition the Angel Theliel. For health matters we can refer to the correspondences of the Planetary Angels (see pages 40–57). Here is a simple blueprint for a petition, which you can apply to any situation:

In the name of the Almighty
(or any other name for God you prefer)
I ask you great Angel ....
To (state wish) ....
I honor you and thank you for receiving my prayer,
As is your holy duty,
In the name of the Almighty (or other title).

Date your petition numerically—for instance, 9.24.2001—and sign it with your usual signature. The rest of the petition should be written in angelic script.

Petitions are traditionally written on squares of plain white paper, or corresponding colored paper in the case of the Planetary Angels. Put your petition in an envelope together with any relevant items, such as a photograph, a flower petal, or a pinch of incense—whatever you feel may help the angels tune in to your request. If your wish is fulfilled or no longer applies, you can burn it with gratitude, thereby dissolving its energy.

Below: Writing a petition to the angel of your choice requires a calm, quiet mind and dedicated concentration in addition to the initial prepraration of items.

Evocation of Hagiel

An evocation differs from an invocation or a petition in that it embodies a request, or a summons, for a specific spirit to manifest before us instead of simply an address to an angel. This is not easy to achieve, and great care must be taken with every aspect of the ritual. Any mistake may result in an unpleasant, possibly dangerous, experience.

From the point of view that sees angels as powerful manifestations of psychic energy, an evocation may be said to be a potentially mind-blowing experience, unleashing, as it does, very powerful energies from the unconscious. From the more literal perspective, one is drawing into a confined space a spiritual being of enormous energy.

May these warnings serve to discourage you from attempting an evocation until you are fully conversant with invocations and petitions; have made successful contact with your personal guardian angel; and have familiarized yourself with the energetic qualities of the angel to be evoked. This ritual evokes the female form of the Angel Hagiel, the Intelligence of Venus, planet of love and affection.

The Ritual

Before attempting this ritual you should have familiarized yourself with it so well that you can visualize everything with your eyes shut. Make a checklist of all the necessary items and have them ready. Purify yourself in advance, as outlined on pages 108–109. The ritual is to be performed on a Friday night at 10 o'clock, the day and hour of Venus.

Put a green lightbulb in the light of the room you will use and sprinkle saltwater around the edges of the room. After bathing, put on a green robe and a copper necklace with a green stone. Anoint your wrists, breast, and temples with apricot oil mixed with a drop each of sandalwood and cinnamon oils.

On the east side of the circle you will make, place a triangle of green silk with equal sides about 18 inches (47 cm) long. On the cloth place a seven-pointed star cut from green card. Make a circle around the cloth (clockwise) with 49 green-colored stones (you can substitute small flour balls made with water, white flour, and green vegetable dye). Forty-nine is Hagiel's number (seven) squared.

Place a green candle at the east, south, west, and north points of this circle. Light them and extinguish all other lights except the green light. Burn some cinnamon and sandalwood. Now face the east, with the cloth a few feet in front of you, and perform the Kabbalistic Cross as explained on pages 110-111. Then perform the Ritual of the Pentagram as explained on pages 111–113, at the end of which you should find yourself facing the east.

Now you may invoke the lovely Angel Hagiel. The invocation is simple: Intone her name silently seven times in your mind (ha–gee–el); then whisper her name seven times; then call her seven times in ringing tones, concluding, equally loud, "Come thou before me!" If you have been in calm, confident command of the whole process up until this point, you should observe a beautiful female form materialize before your eyes.

You will likely be stunned by her presence, but her manner is always sweet and affectionate. Keep control of yourself—remember you are in charge!—and ask her to bestow the gift of unconditional love on the person of your choice. You may now thank her and bid her farewell. She will slowly fade from sight.

If she failed to appear, try again! Remember: it is what you bring, in terms of powerful, confident, contained energy that determines your success in evoking angels.

Right: Make sure you have all the items you need at hand before performing the evocation of hagiel.

Glossary

alchemy An ancient art of spiritual and physical transformation, originating in Egypt.

Annunciation The announcement to the Virgin Mary by the Archangel Gabriel that she had been chosen to bear the Son of God.

Apocrypha 14 books included as an appendix to the Old Testament in Roman Catholicism, but excluded from the Hebrew canon and Protestant versions of the Bible.

Assyria An ancient kingdom of northern Mesopotamia. It became an empire that in the 7th century B.C. stretched from the Persian Gulf to Egypt.

Babylonia The southern kingdom of ancient Mesopotamia. Its empire dominated the region from about 2200–538 B.C., when it was defeated by the Persians.

Buddhism The religion propagated by the followers of the Buddha, (d.483 B.C.), a religious teacher of northern India. It has no god and teaches that perfect enlightenment can be achieved through the abandonment of selfishness and illusion.

Chaldeans An ancient Semitic people who controlled southern Babylonia from the late 8th to late 7th century B.C. They are noted for their knowledge of astrology.

choir Any of the nine orders of angels in medieval angelology.

Enoch An early Hebrew patriarch mentioned in *Genesis* as the father of Methuselah.

equinox The days marking the advent of spring and autumn, when the day and night are of equal length, usually March 20/21 and September 20/21. Celebrated as solar festivals by traditional cultures.

hinduism A system of religious beliefs and social customs, found mainly in India. It requires no one belief concerning the nature of God. Its most famous religious text is the *Bhagavad-Gita*.

invocation The act of calling upon an agent, such as an angel, for assistance.

Islam The religion of the Muslims. A revealed monotheistic faith founded by the Prophet Mohammed in the 7th century A.D. Its sacred scripture is the *Koran*.

jinn (or **genie**) In Islam, an order of spirits lower than angels. They can appear in human or animal form and exert magical influence on people.

Judaism The religion of the Jews, based on a belief in one God, whose will is revealed in the *Torah*. One of the first great monotheistic religions, believing in an all-powerful creator God who consciously administers Creation.

Kabbalah The main tradition of Jewish mysticism, based on the *Sepher Yetzirah* and the *Zohar*, which include esoteric interpretations of the *Torah*. Elements of the *Kabbalah* have greatly influenced western magic and angelology.

Last Judgment According to biblical tradition this event will take place following the Second Coming of Christ and the resurrection of the dead. God will judge all people according to their actions in life and seal their fate accordingly.

Mesopotamia A region of Asia Minor between the rivers Tigris and Euphrates now in modern-day Iraq. Known as the "cradle of western civilization," it spawned the cultures that produced Judaism, Christianity, and Islam.

Moorish Of or relating to the Moors, a North African people of mixed Arab and Berber descent. They converted to Islam in the 8th century and established a powerful empire which included Spain, which they ruled from 756–1492 A.D.

petition A written request for help addressed to a higher authority.

planetary Of or pertaining to the planets of the solar system. The seven "classical" planets include the Sun and the Moon.

Pseudepigrapha Another name for the *Apocrypha*, but including further texts.

Sibylline Oracles A collection of prophetic sayings accorded to the Cumaean sibyl, a prophetess who guided Aeneas, legendary father of the Romans, through the underworld. These oracles contributed to the development of Roman custom, politics, and religion.

Solomon The son of King David, slayer of Goliath. He built the Temple of Jerusalem using sacred and magical means.

solstice The longest and shortest days of the year falling on June 20/21 and December 20/21 respectively. Celebrated as solar festivals by traditional societies. Winter solstice is known as Yule.

spirit A disincarnate being, such as a ghost, angel, or demon.

Sufism The mysticism or esotericism of Islam. Its doctrines and methods are derived from the *Koran* and Islamic revelation.

Sumerian Of or relating to Sumer, a Mesopotamian civilization of the 4th century B.C.

Talmud The main source of Jewish religious law, consisting of two texts, the *Mishnah* and the *Gemara*.

Torah The whole body of traditional Jewish teaching, including the Old Testament and the *Talmud*.

Tree of Life A tree in the Garden of Eden whose fruit gave human beings immortality. In the *Kabbalah* it is a concept expressing the hierarchical nature of the Universe. There are ten interconnected stages (sephiroth), which the initiate attempts to ascend in order to achieve union with the divine.

Zoroaster A Persian prophet of the 6th century B.C., founder of a religion based on the dualistic struggle between good and evil. He was the first prophet to proclaim that salvation is possible for the humble as well as the great of mankind.

Index

Page numbers in *italics* refer to captions

Credits

Quarto would like to thank and acknowledge the following for supplying pictures reproduced in this book:

Key: B = Bottom, T = Top, C = Centre, L = Left, R = Right

Ann Ronan Picture Library: Page 8 L, page 15 R, page 21 R, page 24/25 C, page 24 BL, page 30, page 38 BL, page 39 TR. **Corel Images:** Page 54 TR **Gateshead Council:** Page 6-7. **Images Colour Library:** Page 96 TR. **Superstock:** Page 6 C, page 37 B, Page 101 R. **US Geological Survey:** Page 92 CL.